SCI

WITHDRAWN

LIVING with DIABETES

Also in the Teen's Guides series

Living with Anxiety Disorders
Living with Asthma
Living with Cancer
Living with Depression

teen's guides

LIVING with DIABETES

Katrina Parker, M.D.

SAN DIEGO PUBLIC LIBRARY
TEEN SERVICES

3 1336 08257 5623

An imprint of Infobase Publishing

Living with Diabetes

Copyright © 2008 by Katrina Parker, M.D.

All rights reserved. No part of this book may be reproduced or utilized in any form or by any means, electronic or mechanical, including photocopying, recording, or by any information storage or retrieval systems, without permission in writing from the publisher. For information contact:

Facts On File, Inc.
An imprint of Infobase Publishing
132 West 31st Street
New York NY 10001

Library of Congress Cataloging-in-Publication Data
Parker, Katrina.
Living with diabetes / by Katrina Parker.
p. cm.—(Teen's guides)
Includes bibliographical references and index.
ISBN-13: 978-0-8160-6346-8
ISBN-10: 0-8160-6346-X
1. Diabetes—Juvenile literature. 2. Diabetes in children—
Juvenile literature. I. Title.
RC660.5.B65 2007
616.4'62—dc22 2007027679

Facts On File books are available at special discounts when purchased in bulk quantities for businesses, associations, institutions, or sales promotions. Please call our Special Sales Department in New York at (212) 967-8800 or (800) 322-8755.

You can find Facts On File on the World Wide Web at http://www.factsonfile.com

Text design by Annie O'Donnell
Cover design by Joo Young An

Printed in the United States of America

Sheridan CGI 10 9 8 7 6 5 4 3 2 1

This book is printed on acid-free paper.

CONTENTS

Prediabetes: On the Edge

Jenny was just 16 when she started feeling thirsty all the time. She spent hours eating snacks while surfing the Net and messaging her friends on her computer, and she'd gained about 25 pounds since she entered adolescence. When her pediatrician noted her blood pressure inching upward, Jenny's mom mentioned her daughter's constant thirst. Jenny's grandmother and two aunts had diabetes, and her mom worried that Jenny also was developing the disease. Not surprisingly, tests showed that Jenny had what's called prediabetes—her blood sugar was higher than normal yet not quite high enough for an official diagnosis of diabetes. Most people with prediabetes go on to develop full-blown Type 2 diabetes within 10 years. *Diabetes* is a collective term for a group of diseases involving problems with how the body produces and uses a hormone called insulin.

Every day more and more young Americans (even elementary schoolers) are being diagnosed with prediabetes, which is linked to obesity, poor diet, high blood pressure, and lack of exercise. The rise in prediabetes is linked to the rise in the number of kids starting to have weight problems. In 2000, 22 percent of the nation's preschoolers were overweight, and 10 percent were clinically obese. Furthermore, one recent study found that 25 percent of very obese children and 21 percent of very obese teenagers had prediabetes.

Therefore, you can think of a diagnosis of prediabetes as a wake-up call. Once you know you have this condition, you can start losing extra weight and getting more exercise to try to prevent the development of diabetes later in your life. Research shows that losing weight and exercising more can help prevent Type 2 diabetes in both kids and adults, and it's important to do everything you can to prevent the disease from developing.

Diabetes affects how the body processes glucose, a kind of simple sugar that the body uses for fuel. Just like a car that needs gas to run, your body needs sugar to function. When you eat a cheeseburger for lunch, your body removes sugar from the food and sends it into your bloodstream. At the same time, your pancreas makes a hormone called insulin, which acts like a key to help unlock your body's cells so sugar can enter. Sugar provides the energy you need to shoot hoops, play the piano, or think of the answers to that geometry problem.

There are two main types of diabetes: Type 1 and Type 2. Each affects insulin differently, but both result in high blood sugar levels. As the doctor explained to Jenny, Type 1 diabetes (also called juvenile diabetes or insulin-dependent diabetes) occurs when the body stops producing insulin. If you have Type 1 diabetes, your body can still break down sugar from food, but without insulin, the sugar can't get into the cells. Instead, it floats around in the blood, raises your blood sugar level very high, and causes health problems. Most experts believe that Type 1 diabetes is an autoimmune disease—a condition in which your immune system mistakenly attacks your body. Once a person has Type 1 diabetes, the body can't ever produce insulin again. That's why people with Type 1 diabetes must get insulin from daily shots or an insulin pump. It's not true that eating too much sugar causes diabetes, so you can't prevent Type 1 diabetes, no matter how much you avoid sugar.

Type 2 diabetes is usually a preventable condition that occurs when the body loses the ability to use insulin efficiently. Weight gain, poor nutrition, and lack of exercise reduce the action of insulin. At first, the body makes up for this by boosting production of insulin, but eventually the pancreas just can't keep up, and blood sugar begins to rise. This eventually leads to Type 2 diabetes. Until not very long ago, Type 2 diabetes was usually diagnosed in adults over age 30. Recently, research has reported that the rate of Type 2 diabetes among children worldwide has been on the rise for the last 15 years. Unlike Type I, you can prevent Type 2 diabetes by watching your diet and your weight.

WHY SHOULD YOU BE WORRIED ABOUT PREDIABETES?

Because having prediabetes means you don't have diabetes yet, you may wonder what the big deal is. Prediabetes is a serious problem because most people who have it go on to develop Type 2 diabetes. People with prediabetes also are at higher risk of developing heart disease, and some studies suggest that once you've got prediabetes, your heart and circulatory system may have already sustained damage.

The increasing risk of diabetes is startling: Experts predict that one out of three Americans born in 2000 will develop diabetes during his or her lifetime, an estimated lifetime risk of about 33 percent for men and 39 percent for women. Government statistics predict that if things don't change, these figures will increase 165 percent by the year 2050.

SYMPTOMS OF PREDIABETES

Unfortunately, you may have prediabetes and not know it because you have no symptoms or symptoms develop so slowly you just don't notice. Symptoms of prediabetes and diabetes include:

- unusual thirst
- a frequent desire to urinate
- blurred vision
- fatigue for no apparent reason
- unexplained weight loss

WHO'S AT RISK?

There are many risk factors for developing prediabetes and Type 2 diabetes. Some you can control, and some you can't. The risks you can't control include:

- family history of Type 2 diabetes; a child with one parent with Type 2 diabetes has about a 25 percent chance of getting it, and a child with two affected parents has a 50 percent risk
- belonging to an ethnic group at high risk for diabetes, such as African Americans, Asian Americans/Pacific Islanders, Latinos, and Native Americans

Online Risk Test

The American Diabetes Association offers an online "risk test" for you to figure out if you're at higher risk for developing diabetes. To take the test, visit: http://www.diabetes.org/risk-test.jsp.

The risks you can control are related to your diet and lifestyle, and include:

- high blood pressure
- low HDL (the "good") cholesterol
- high triglycerides (a type of fat in the blood)
- eating large portions of high-fat, high-calorie foods and a lot of fast food
- not getting any exercise

HOW IS DIABETES DIAGNOSED?

In 2000, the American Academy of Pediatrics recommended that doctors test obese children for diabetes if they have at least two of the risk factors for prediabetes. If you have some of these symptoms or you're at high risk for developing diabetes, your doctor will probably give you one of two tests:

- ***Fasting plasma glucose test (FPG):*** This test measures your blood sugar first thing in the morning, before you eat anything.
- ***Oral glucose tolerance test (OGTT):*** This test measures your blood sugar after fasting and again two hours later after drinking a sugary beverage.

A normal blood sugar level after fasting is below 100 milligrams per deciliter (mg/dl). If you have prediabetes, your fasting level will be between 100 and 125 mg/dl. If your level tops 126 mg/dl, you have diabetes.

Doctors sometimes call prediabetes impaired glucose tolerance or impaired fasting glucose, depending on which test was used to diagnose the problem. In any case, if you have prediabetes, you should be checked for Type 2 diabetes every one or two years.

Microalbumin test. Anyone who develops diabetes after puberty should have a microalbumin urine test once a year. This test assesses your risk for developing kidney or artery disease by checking for small amounts of protein in the urine that can't be detected by routine urinalysis. The test uses specialized dipsticks or urine collections over a period of 12 to 24 hours. Persistent microalbumin over several repeated tests at different times suggests a higher risk for macrovascular and kidney disease.

TREATING PREDIABETES

You won't need to take insulin if you have prediabetes, but you'll need to get serious about making some important lifestyle changes. Studies of both kids and adults have now shown that about 58 percent of all Type 2 diabetes may be prevented or at least delayed by eating less and exercising more. According to a 2004 study of children in Germany, significant weight loss through a healthy diet and regular physical activity can improve insulin sensitivity in overweight children and teens.

Eat more healthfully. Experts recommend that if you have prediabetes, you should drop your weight by 5 to 10 percent. If you weigh 140 pounds, you need to lose about seven to 14 pounds. You don't have to pay lots of money to go to a fancy weight-loss clinic or buy lots of expensive special foods. If you just eat less and eat healthier foods, you should lose weight. You'll learn more about healthy diets in chapter 6, but here are some suggestions to help you:

1. Eat smaller portions. Portion size in the United States is way out of control. Most restaurants serve far more food than you should really be eating. Avoid all-you-can-eat buffets and super-sized meals.
2. No fad diets. Aim for eating all kinds of healthy foods in moderation. Choose lean meats, whole grains, and fresh fruits and vegetables; you can have an occasional piece of pie, a small soda, or a bit of chocolate as an occasional treat.
3. Avoid soda. Did you know there are at least 12 teaspoons of sugar in one regular size soda? There are lots of calories hiding in many types of beverages (other than water). Either drink water or low-calorie beverages or consume fewer high-calorie drinks.
4. Cut out the fat. Don't eat lots of butter or fried foods and you'll eliminate a lot of fat; instead, bake or broil your meat. Drink low-fat milk instead of whole or 2 percent.
5. Eat healthful snacks. Reach for fresh fruits and vegetables; if you don't like cooked vegetables, try eating the same foods your family is eating, but make yours raw. Some kids swear that raw peas, carrots, broccoli, and peppers are much tastier.

Exercise! You also need to get up from the couch, put down your computer mouse, and get some mild physical exercise—at least 30 minutes a day, five days a week. (Even a half hour three days a week is better than nothing, though!) If you do this, you may actually get your blood sugar levels back to normal. Try to limit yourself to no more than two hours in front of the computer and TV screen a day.

Don't like to exercise? You don't have to do jumping jacks and push-ups. Try walking around the block or get out your bike. Play Frisbee with your friends. Turn to chapter 7 for more details on healthy exercising.

Avoid bad habits. Because people with prediabetes have a 50 percent higher risk of heart disease and stroke, make sure you don't start smoking or quit if you've already started. You also should watch your blood pressure and cholesterol.

WHAT YOU NEED TO KNOW

- *Diabetes* is a collective term for a group of diseases involving problems with how the body produces and uses a hormone called insulin.
- There are two main types of diabetes: Type 1 and Type 2. Type 1 diabetes usually affects children and occurs when the body stops producing insulin. Type 2 diabetes occurs when the body can't efficiently use the insulin it does produce.
- Prediabetes is a condition in which the blood sugar is higher than normal, yet not quite high enough for an official diagnosis of diabetes.
- Most people with prediabetes go on to develop full-blown Type 2 diabetes within 10 years.
- Prediabetes is linked to obesity, poor diet, high blood pressure, and lack of exercise.
- People with prediabetes can prevent the development of Type 2 diabetes by getting more exercise and losing weight.
- Symptoms of diabetes include unusual thirst, a frequent desire to urinate, blurred vision, fatigue for no apparent reason, and unexplained weight loss.
- Diabetes is diagnosed by either a fasting plasma glucose test (FPG) or an oral glucose tolerance test (OGTT).
- Prediabetes is not treated with insulin but with good diet and lots of exercise.

2

All About Type 1 and Type 2 Diabetes

Everybody has some amount of sugar in their blood— it provides the fuel for your body—but too much can cause lots of problems. You know that you need to eat and drink to provide energy for your body to function. To understand diabetes, however, you really need to know how your body uses food, which is called the metabolic process. First, food provides fuel, not just to power your brain and every living cell in your body, but to build new tissue and repair damage and regulate all your body's functions. Before your body can use the food you eat, however, it must be broken down into smaller parts. When you take a bite of a cheeseburger, your body gets right to work breaking down the beef, the cheese, and the bun into proteins, carbohydrates, and fats. Hamburger is full of protein (as are fish, milk, and nuts). The cheese is a fat, which is also found in oils, butter, dairy products, and meat. Carbs (also called starches or sugars) include the burger bun, along with other breads, pasta, fruits, and veggies. Your body breaks down carbohydrates into glucose (or simple sugar) that moves through your intestinal walls into your blood, where it's called "blood glucose" or "blood sugar."

Many of the foods you probably love—such as pasta and candy—contain carbohydrates that the body turns into blood sugar. Although all carbs raise blood sugar levels, some are better choices than others because they're more nutritious. For example, sweets have concentrated simple sugars, but typically have fewer vitamins, minerals, protein, fiber, and other nutrients commonly found in fruits and vegetables.

INSULIN ENTERS THE PICTURE

Your blood carries this blood sugar to all the cells in your body, where insulin made by your pancreas helps it enter the cells, particularly those of your muscles and liver. Normally, your muscles and other body tissues work together with insulin as a team to help move sugar out of the bloodstream and into the cells. Only a small amount of insulin is needed to do this job. But if your body doesn't make enough insulin or if the insulin doesn't work correctly, the blood sugar can't get into your cells. As a result, it builds up in your blood until the sugar level gets dangerously high, starving the cells of energy and inducing a life-threatening coma.

TYPE 1 V. TYPE 2

There are two main types of diabetes—Type 1 and Type 2. Type 1 is almost always diagnosed in childhood (which is why it's also known as juvenile diabetes). Type 2 is the result of poor diet and exercise and can be diagnosed at any age.

Type 1 diabetes. Every day, another 35 children in the United States are diagnosed with Type 1 diabetes, which occurs when the body stops producing insulin. If you have this form of diabetes, your body can still break down sugar from food, but without insulin, the blood sugar can't enter your cells. Instead, it floats around in your blood, raising your blood sugar level too high and causing health problems. Once Type 1 diabetes develops, the body can never produce insulin again. That's why people with Type 1 diabetes must get insulin from daily injections or an insulin pump. Because Type 1 diabetes is probably caused by a malfunction in the immune system, no matter how much sugar you avoid or how much you change your lifestyle, you can't prevent it.

Type 1 diabetes is divided into two forms: immune-mediated diabetes (Type 1A) and idiopathic diabetes (Type 1B). Type 1A is caused by the destruction of the insulin-producing beta cells of the pancreas. Markers for the immune destruction of the beta cells include the presence of antibodies, which are found in between 85 and 90 percent of individuals when fasting high blood sugar levels are diagnosed.

Diabetes Type 1B has no known cause, although it appears to be inherited. Some patients with this form have permanent insulin deficiency and are prone to ketoacidosis, but there isn't any evidence that their immune systems have attacked beta cells. Although this form of diabetes is rare, those who have it are primarily of African, Hispanic, or Asian descent. Individuals with this form of diabetes experience

Maturity-Onset Diabetes of the Young (MODY)

This fairly rare form of diabetes occurs early in life (before age 25) and is inherited (each child of an affected parent has a 50 percent chance of getting this disease). In addition, there is typically diabetes in at least two generations of the patient's family. MODY affects only about 2 percent of all diabetes patients.

MODY can often be controlled by diet or oral medication, at least in the early stages. However, it differs from Type 2 diabetes because MODY patients have a defect in insulin secretion or glucose metabolism—they are not resistant to insulin.

So far, six genes have been found that cause MODY, although not all patients have one of these genes.

varying degrees of insulin deficiency between episodes, and so their need for insulin replacement therapy may come and go.

Type 2 diabetes. In Type 2 diabetes, which can be prevented through proper diet and exercise, the body loses the ability to efficiently use insulin produced by the pancreas. More and more insulin is required to move normal amounts of sugar into the cells. This causes the pancreas to produce more insulin. Doctors call this change in the tissue insulin resistance. Weight gain, poor nutrition, and lack of exercise can all trigger insulin resistance. Your pancreas may be able to make more insulin to keep sugar moving from the blood into your tissues for a time, but eventually it just can't keep up, and the amount of blood sugar rises, causing Type 2 diabetes. In the past, Type 2 diabetes was usually diagnosed in adults over age 30, but studies show that the rate of Type 2 diabetes among children around the world has risen for the last 15 years.

DO YOU HAVE ANY OF THESE SYMPTOMS?

Symptoms of Type 1 and Type 2 diabetes are similar, but symptoms of Type 2 diabetes develop much more slowly. Kids with Type 1 diabetes often experience symptoms so noticeable that they go to their doctor right away. The following are symptoms of either type of diabetes:

- constant excessive thirst
- frequent urination
- extreme hunger
- fatigue
- unexplained weight loss
- blurry vision

The primary symptoms of diabetes are related to the problems of insulin and excessive blood sugar.

Thirst. High levels of blood sugar trigger your kidneys to pump out more urine in an effort to remove excess sugar. As more urine is produced and expelled, your body becomes dehydrated and needs more water, triggering feelings of thirst.

Urination. Your body's effort to pump out more urine to dilute the amount of sugar in your blood means you're constantly running to the bathroom. Unfortunately, this isn't a very effective way of normalizing blood sugar levels.

Hunger. Your body has lots of ways to compensate for problems. As it gets harder and harder for blood sugar to enter your cells, they start to feel deprived. Your body interprets this as starvation and triggers your brain to set off hunger signals so you'll eat more. Your body "thinks" this will satisfy its cells, not realizing that the problem isn't that you're not eating but that an insulin problem is preventing sugar from getting into your cells.

Tiredness. Your body needs sugar to function, and if blood sugar isn't reaching your cells, they're running on empty. Since blood sugar is the primary fuel (especially for your brain), you start to lose energy and feel sluggish as diabetes develops.

Weight loss. People with diabetes, especially Type 1, tend to lose weight because their cells aren't getting the sugar they need, and so the body turns to its fat and protein stores for fuel.

Blurry vision. Diabetes causes a lot of problems with the eyes. Temporary blurry vision occurs when your body dehydrates because you're urinating more, which allows the lens of the eye to dry up and shrivel. At the same time, too much blood sugar can make the lens in your eye swell, which also blurs your vision.

TYPE 1 DIABETES: CAUSES AND RISK FACTORS

Doctors don't know how to prevent Type I diabetes or predict who's going to get it. In fact, doctors aren't even sure what causes Type 1 diabetes, though they do know what *doesn't* cause it. You won't get Type 1 diabetes because you ate too many Mallomars, too much fast food, or drank too much soda. Even if you binge on cake, cookies, and chocolate bars, a healthy pancreas can produce enough insulin to process all that sugar pouring into your blood. Diabetes isn't contagious; nor can you get it from a blood transfusion. It's not your fault if you have Type 1 diabetes.

So, what causes the problem? Type 1 diabetes occurs when your immune system attacks your pancreas and destroys the cells that make insulin. Heredity plays a role. If one of your parents has Type 1 diabetes, your risk is between 5 and 10 percent, which rises to 20 percent if both your parents have it. On the other hand, up to 85 percent of people with Type 1 diabetes have no family history of the disease.

Genes. Some evidence suggests that a number of genes that help the body tell the difference between toxic invaders and normal body tissues may be involved in Type 1 diabetes. For example, almost all people with this condition have a particular type of immune system gene called the *DR3* form of *human leukocyte antigen (HLA)* genes. There are, however, many people who have these genes but don't have diabetes.

Race. Caucasians are more likely to develop Type 1 diabetes, especially those from Scandinavia or other countries in northern Europe. It's also common in colder climates and develops more often in winter than in summer. Asians, Native Americans, and Africans rarely develop Type 1 diabetes.

Age. It's most common to develop Type 1 diabetes in childhood and adolescence; it's rare for anyone over age 30 to suddenly be diagnosed with this problem. The period of highest risk occurs between ages 11 and 14; the diagnosis declines after puberty sets in.

Viruses. Some experts suspect that viruses may play a role in triggering the onset of Type 1 diabetes. They think this because many kids who are diagnosed with the condition have recently recovered from a viral infection (especially mumps or measles). This could also explain why more cases are diagnosed in the winter when more viruses are present.

This form of diabetes is certainly a serious condition that must be treated, but a diagnosis now is not as negative as it was in the past. Today, there are more choices for blood sugar testing and insulin treatment than ever, and new developments are occurring all the time. With proper daily care and treatment, children and teens with Type 1 diabetes can lead healthy, active lives.

TYPE 2 DIABETES: CAUSES AND RISK FACTORS

It used to take years for a person to develop insulin resistance, which is why Type 2 diabetes was diagnosed mostly in adulthood after age 40. An alarming new trend in America, fueled by lack of exercise, poor diet, and obesity, is more frequent diagnoses of Type 2 diabetes in 'tweens and teens. Ten years ago, a child with Type 2 diabetes would have been so unusual that the case probably would have been written up in a medical journal. Today, it's becoming all too common. In fact, Type 2 diabetes in teens now represents one of the most rapidly growing forms of diabetes in the United States and perhaps the world.

More than 90 percent of all people with diabetes have Type 2 diabetes, and there are four uncontrollable factors that put people at higher risk for developing it: race, family history, the onset of puberty, and gender.

Race. Certain ethnic groups appear to have a higher risk of developing Type 2 diabetes, whether they are overweight or not. These groups include Africans, Hispanics, Native Americans, Pacific Islanders, and Southern Asians. For example, although the overall prevalence of Type 2 diabetes in the United States is 6 percent, about 50 percent of all the Pima Indians in Arizona have it.

Genes. While obesity is one of the major risk factors for Type 2 diabetes, not all obese people develop the disease nor are all Type 2 diabetics overweight. That's why scientists know other factors are also involved in the development of this form of diabetes. Although the risk for the general population is about 6 percent, people who have a parent or sibling with the disease have an increased risk of about 10 to 15 percent. If that sibling is an identical twin, the risk rises to almost 100 percent. (This risk may not be entirely genetic; Type 2 diabetes is also triggered by obesity, and twins may share a strong lifestyle similarity that puts them at similar risk.)

Doctors have long recognized that Type 2 diabetes seems to run in families. Now scientists have discovered several gene variations they think might play a role in this condition. In fact, some scientists think that specific variations of a gene may cause up to 20 percent of all Type 2 diabetes cases. However, it hasn't been easy to find the genes responsible. Controlling metabolism and food involves many genes. A mutation in one probably would not cause diabetes, but mutations in several could add up to a higher risk.

Scientists have discovered several gene mutations that affect a protein that regulates insulin activity. If your body makes a lot of this protein, your ability to respond to insulin would be blunted, which would lead to higher sugar in your bloodstream.

Genes are not the only culprits. Lifestyle and environment play a large role in whether or not someone will develop Type 2 diabetes. Two people may have the same gene mutations, but if one person controls her weight and exercises regularly, she may not develop diabetes.

Because the genetics of Type 2 diabetes is so complicated, with many different genes influencing your risk, Type 2 diabetes is not inherited in a clearly dominant or recessive way. Instead, you may inherit one gene that increases your risk, and other genes that lower your risk. Together, these genes—along with your diet, weight, and exercise level—determine your overall risk of developing Type 2 diabetes.

Because there are so many variables to consider, it will probably be a long time before any kind of genetic test is available for Type 2 diabetes. For now the American Academy of Pediatrics recommends that doctors test you for diabetes if you're overweight and you have at least two of the risk factors for diabetes. The American Diabetes Association recommends screening for diabetes onset every three years if you have diabetes in the family.

Puberty. The onset of puberty may play a major role in the development of Type 2 diabetes in teens. Everyone becomes more insulin resistant during puberty, but recently, more and more teens don't seem able to compensate for this resistance.

Gender. There is a slightly higher risk for girls and women to develop Type 2 diabetes.

Preventable causes. More and more younger people are developing this preventable form of diabetes because of poor diet, obesity, and lack of exercise, all of which you can do something about. If there were no obesity, Type 2 diabetes, the most common form of the disease, would be rare.

WHY DIABETES IS SO SERIOUS

Having high blood sugar as a result of either type of diabetes is associated with a number of long-term medical complications. High blood sugar can damage small blood vessels, leading to blindness, kidney damage, and earlier development of hardening of the arteries (called atherosclerosis) that contributes to heart attacks and stroke. Type 1 diabetes can damage nerves throughout the body, possibly leading to amputation of injured limbs. We'll discuss more about the complications of diabetes in chapter 9. The good news is that research studies have shown that the development of these complications may be delayed or prevented if you can maintain control of blood sugar levels over time.

THE NEXT STEP

Okay, you've been diagnosed with diabetes (either Type 1 or 2). The next step is to start taking good care of yourself and to learn how to manage all aspects of your diabetes. You'll learn how to manage the food you eat, the exercise you get, and, in some cases, the medicines you take. This will help your body stabilize blood sugar, and you'll end up feeling better and avoiding the long-term complications of diabetes.

WHAT YOU NEED TO KNOW

- Your body gets sugar from the food you eat and carries this sugar in your blood to all the cells in your body, where insulin made by your pancreas helps it enter the cells.
- If the body doesn't make enough insulin or if the insulin doesn't work correctly, sugar can't get into the cells and builds up in the blood to dangerously high levels; the cells become starved for energy, and a person can go into a life-threatening coma.
- In Type 1 diabetes, the body can't produce insulin and must get insulin from daily injections or an insulin pump.
- In Type 2 diabetes, the body loses the ability to use insulin efficiently, so that more and more insulin is needed to move

sugar into the cells. This causes the pancreas to create more insulin. Doctors call this insulin resistance.

- Symptoms for Types 1 and 2 are similar (but Type 2 develops more slowly) and include constant excessive thirst, frequent urination, extreme hunger, fatigue, unexplained weight loss, and blurry vision.
- Type 1 diabetes occurs when the immune system attacks the pancreas and destroys the cells that make insulin. It can't be prevented.
- The chance of developing Type 2 diabetes is influenced by race, gender, heredity, puberty, and lifestyle (not enough exercise and too much unhealthy food).
- Diabetes is serious because high blood sugar can damage small blood vessels, leading to blindness, kidney damage, and the earlier development of hardening of the arteries. Type 1 diabetes can damage nerves throughout the body, eventually leading to possible amputation of injured limbs.

3

Managing Diabetes: The Basics of High and of Low Blood Sugar

Not so very long ago, doctors thought that all of the scary complications of diabetes—blindness, kidney failure, and nerve damage—were unavoidable parts of the disease. Today, we know that with good control of blood sugar levels, those complications can be lessened or completely avoided. The Diabetes Control and Complications Trial in 1993 proved that keeping blood sugar levels under tight control could prevent or at least slow down the development of many of the complications of diabetes, giving people many extra years of healthy, active life.

That's a real incentive for taking as good care of yourself as possible. Now that you've been diagnosed with diabetes, your immediate goal should be to keep on doing the things you've always enjoyed doing while keeping your blood sugar controlled. Usually, this means keeping most of your blood sugar test results in a range between 80 to 180 milligrams per deciliter (80 to 180 mg/dl). Life with diabetes does require a lot of planning and preparation, but you can still have lots of fun and keep doing everything you've always enjoyed. Diabetes doesn't have to stop you from living a normal, full life.

YOUR PERSONAL DIABETES PLAN

Your diabetes specialist can help you develop a personal diabetes plan and discuss ways to manage low blood sugar (hypoglycemia) and high blood sugar (hyperglycemia). Your Diabetes Medical Management Plan (DMMP) will help you maintain a daily schedule to keep your diabetes under control. The plan shows you how to follow a healthy meal plan, get regular physical activity, check your blood sugar levels, and take insulin or oral medication as prescribed.

Eat healthfully. An important part of managing your diabetes is following a meal plan developed by your doctor, diabetes educator, or dietician. We'll discuss your diet more thoroughly in chapter 6, but basically, your meal plan will outline proper nutrition so you continue to grow while keeping your blood sugar in the target range. In the next chapter, you'll learn how different types of food, especially carbohydrates such as breads, pasta, and rice, can affect your blood sugar levels. We'll also discuss portion size, the right amount of calories for your age and size, and ideas for healthy food choices.

Get off the couch. All kids need exercise, but if you have diabetes it's even more important. Exercise helps to lower blood sugar levels, especially if you have Type 2 diabetes. Exercise is also a good way to help control your weight. We'll discuss exercise more thoroughly in chapter 7, but, in general, you should check your blood sugar levels before you start playing a sport or being active. You shouldn't exercise if your blood sugar levels are too low.

Check blood sugar levels. You should check your blood sugar levels regularly with a blood glucose meter (a meter with a built-in memory is best). Your diabetes specialist will show you how to use a blood glucose meter properly and discuss how often to use it. In general, food makes blood sugar go up, and exercise and insulin make blood sugar levels drop. That's why maintaining good blood sugar control isn't always as easy as it may seem at first. It's pretty much a constant juggling act 24 hours a day, seven days a week. Your blood glucose meter will show you if your blood sugar levels are on target or are too high or too low. You should keep a record of your blood sugar results so you can discuss them with your diabetes specialist. This will help your doctor know if he or she needs to make any changes in your personal diabetes plan.

Take your medication. Always take all your diabetes medication as prescribed. If you've got Type 1 diabetes, you need to take your insulin shots at regular times each day. Some kids prefer an insulin pump, which delivers insulin automatically and eliminates the need for shots. Kids with Type 2 diabetes may need oral medication, insulin shots, or both. In any case, you'll need to balance your medication with food and activity every day.

CHECKING YOUR BLOOD SUGAR LEVELS

The first thing to do is learn how to test your blood sugar each day. There are three main variables that affect your blood glucose levels: diet, activity, and insulin. In addition, normal hormonal changes during adolescence can lead to unstable blood sugar. To control your diabetes and prevent complications, your blood sugar levels must be as close to a normal range as possible.

While everyone who takes insulin must regularly check their blood sugar levels, checking is just as important for kids with Type 2 diabetes. That's because some oral medications for Type 2 diabetes can cause low blood sugar. Plus, regular blood sugar checking can help you realize if you need to change your treatment. To check your blood sugar levels, you will need a blood glucose meter.

What kind of meter to get. Blood glucose meters allow users to check and monitor their blood sugar level. They generally require users to prick their skin to draw a drop of blood to place on a test strip, although some combine extraction with testing. They come in all sizes. Smaller meters may be more convenient to carry around, but they require more nimble fingers to use. Look at the test strips too. Is the packaging easy to open and use? Not all strips are user-friendly. Check out how much blood is needed and whether or not the strips need to be wiped. (Some strips require that you apply blood to the test strip, wipe it off at 30 seconds, and read the results at 60 seconds.)

Some new, expensive meters that store a certain number of blood sugar results in memory (anywhere from a few to 250 readings) can be really helpful while you're testing at school. You can even buy meters with sophisticated data management systems that track a variety of aspects of care that can be downloaded into your computer. Many meters can display languages other than English.

Strip Safety

Remember to keep your blood test strips in their original container or vial and not in a plastic bag, which could make them deteriorate.

Some aspects of buying a meter will be up to your parents. Some insurance companies only cover certain meters and may not pay for more expensive models; other models may be more reasonable, but have very expensive test strips. Since you're the one who will be using the meter, see if you and your parents can go meter shopping together to choose the best product for you.

How often to check. How often you check your blood levels could change from day to day. Your doctor or diabetes educator will discuss with you when and how often to check on a normal day. Doctors typically recommend that students check their blood sugar during the school day, usually before eating snacks or lunch, before physical activity, or when there are symptoms of high or low blood sugar. Although three or four times a day is usually recommended for kids who take insulin, you'll need to check more often when you're sick or when your diabetes treatment or daily habits change. For example, if you join the basketball team, you may have to check a little more often during the first weeks of practice. The extra check can tell you if you need to adjust your food or insulin to balance the higher level of exercise.

Your target levels. You and your parents must work with your diabetes specialist to determine what your target blood sugar levels are. The recommended blood sugar levels for most people with diabetes are from about 80 to 120 before a meal, 180 or less after a meal, and between 100 and 140 at bedtime.

One of the reasons you check your blood sugar levels several times a day is to find out how often blood sugar is in the target range. Your target range is probably slightly different than other kids you may know who have diabetes. That's because it's designed to match your very own needs and lifestyle. Your target range will probably change as you grow or if your diabetes treatment changes.

How to check. To check your blood sugar level, prick the skin with a lancet at the fingertip, forearm, or somewhere else on your body to obtain a drop of blood. Place the drop on a special test strip, which is then inserted in a glucose meter. The meter gives you a reading of your current blood sugar level. Here's how the process works:

1. Wash and dry your hands.
2. Prepare the glucose meter. Each meter works a little differently, so you'll need to read the instructions carefully.

The first time you use it, you practice under the supervision of the doctor or diabetes educator.

3. Choose the spot that you'll prick. Remember, don't check on the same finger all the time or it will get too sore. Instead, select a different finger every time you check.
4. Aim for the side of the fingertip, not right on top where it's more sensitive. Not only will pricking the side hurt less, but it's less likely to bruise.
5. Prepare the finger-prick device. Each device is different, so read the instructions and follow them carefully.
6. Place the device against your finger and push the button.
7. Squeeze out a drop of blood. If it's hard to get a drop, hang your hand down and gently shake or squeeze the finger. If you often have trouble getting a drop of blood, ask your doctor to recommend a different type of finger-pricking device.
8. Place the drop of blood on a test strip and place the test strip in the meter according to the directions.
9. Record the results.

Keeping records. Keeping records is one of the most important parts of managing diabetes. You've got to test your levels and track them so that you know how much insulin you need.

Is your meter accurate? Accuracy is very important when checking your blood sugar levels. To make sure the meter is accurate, you should calibrate it carefully according to the manufacturer's instructions. If you suspect there's a problem with the meter, ask your doctor if the two of you can compare readings. To do this, take two samples of your blood at the doctor's office. Check one sample on your meter, as usual; the other sample should be checked using the doctor's equipment or sent to a lab for testing. If the result from your meter is more than 20 percent different from the doctor's result, it's time to check the meter.

MINIMALLY INVASIVE AND NONINVASIVE BLOOD SUGAR MONITORING

Nobody likes constantly having to prick their skin to check their blood, and researchers have been spending a lot of time trying to come up with alternatives. So far, the government has approved one minimally invasive meter and one noninvasive meter—but neither of these can be used alone. You still need to combine these with standard blood sugar testing. The new types of monitoring device are used to obtain extra sugar values between finger-stick tests. Both devices require daily calibration using standard finger-stick sugar measurements.

Noninvasive method. The Cygnus GlucoWatch Biographer is worn on the wrist like a watch. Without puncturing the skin, the watch measures sugar by pulling tiny amounts of fluid from the skin using a mild electric current. You need to wear the watch for three hours before it's ready to measure; after that, it monitors sugar levels every 20 minutes for 12 hours. If blood sugar levels fall too low or rise too high, the watch will sound an alarm. However, the U.S. Food and Drug Administration cautions that the watch appears less effective in detecting very low glucose levels. Although you must continue to use the finger-stick method along with this device, the watch will lower the number of times a day you have to prick your finger to test your blood sugar levels.

You can read the results yourself, but these readings can't replace finger-stick tests. Instead, these results are meant to show trends and patterns in your sugar levels rather than report any one result alone. It's helpful in evaluating episodes of both hyperglycemia and hypoglycemia. However, you still must confirm results with your regular glucose meter. The GlucoWatch is available by prescription only.

Minimally invasive method. The MiniMed Continuous Glucose Monitoring System consists of a very small plastic tube inserted just under the skin that collects small amounts of liquid, passing it through a sensor to measure the amount of sugar. This device is intended to detect daily blood sugar trends—it won't provide individual readings and therefore can't be used for day-to-day monitoring. After 72 hours of measurements, you or your doctor must download the data for interpretation. Understanding trends over time might help you figure out the best time to do your standard finger-stick tests. MiniMed is also available only by prescription.

Even newer technology. Scientists are constantly studying new noninvasive methods for blood sugar monitoring. One of the newest is designed to painlessly measure blood sugar by shining a beam of light on the skin. Other new methods currently being studied include measuring the energy waves emitted by the body, applying radio waves to the fingertips, ultrasound, and checking the thickness of fluids in tissue underneath the skin.

HYPOGLYCEMIA

No matter how hard you try to keep your blood sugar levels within the target range, they will sometimes spike or drop. When your blood sugar levels drop too low, it leads to a condition called hypoglycemia, which is one of the most frequent complications of diabetes. Taking too much insulin is the most common cause of hypoglycemia, which is why it's sometimes called an insulin reaction. Using fast-acting insulin can increase your risk of low blood sugar because the insulin's effectiveness may peak before your digestion is finished. Slower acting insulin also can cause hypoglycemia if you take too much or don't eat enough during the insulin's peak activity.

Other causes of low sugar levels include forgetting or delaying a meal or snack, not eating enough, or exercising too much or too long. Drinking alcohol is another cause, because alcohol interferes with the liver's response to low blood sugar. Recovering from a serious illness or surgery also can trigger low blood sugar because of the increased energy demands on your body.

In order to function, your brain needs a constant supply of blood sugar. If your blood sugar level drops below 60 mg/dl, your brain will face an emergency situation. You'll need to raise your blood sugar levels *right away.* A low blood sugar level can be life-threatening, and it's the greatest immediate danger to kids with diabetes. It's more likely to happen right before lunch, at the end of school, or during or after physical education.

It's also not that unusual. If you have Type 1 diabetes, you may experience mild hypoglycemia (between 50 and 60 mg/dl) as often as once or twice a week. But remember that the specific blood sugar level reading is *less* important than symptoms when treating hypoglycemia, especially in kids. It's possible to be severely hypoglycemic even if the numbers aren't really low, so *always* treat hypoglycemia by the symptoms.

Mild to moderate symptoms of hypoglycemia. Mild hypoglycemia is 50 to 60 mg/dl; moderate hypoglycemia is 20 to 50 mg/dl. Symptoms of hypoglycemia can be different for different kids and may even vary from episode to episode. When your body senses that your blood sugar levels are dropping, it tries to correct the problem by sending adrenaline (also called epinephrine) to the liver to prompt it to release more sugar. Adrenaline is one of your "fight or flight" stress hormones that you normally experience if you're scared or in danger and need to run away. It's the release of adrenaline that causes the symptoms of hypoglycemia, which may include:

- anxiety (feeling something isn't right)
- feeling cold
- hunger
- rapid heartbeat
- shakiness
- sudden sweating

As your blood sugar levels continue to drop, symptoms continue:

- blurry vision
- concentration problems
- confusion
- disorientation
- dizziness
- headache
- irritability
- lethargy
- pallor
- personality changes (a person may get belligerent, argumentative, or even insist that there's nothing wrong)
- sleepiness
- slurred speech
- uncoordination
- weakness

Treating mild/moderate hypoglycemia. Luckily, hypoglycemia can be treated easily and effectively. Although it is a serious health risk, it is normally more unpleasant than anything else, affecting your judgment, your thinking, and even your balance and ability to walk. But don't ignore it. If hypoglycemia is not treated promptly, it can lead to unconsciousness and convulsions. In rare cases, it can be life threatening.

As soon as you realize you're experiencing hypoglycemia—or as soon as someone else recognizes it—you should eat or drink a quick-acting sugar product equaling 15 grams of carbohydrate. This might be either four ounces of fruit juice; six ounces (usually half a can) of *non-diet* soda; candy, such as six jelly beans, 10 gumdrops, or eight Life Savers; six saltines; two tablespoons of raisins; four packets of

Warning!

If you're experiencing any symptoms of low blood sugar, you should never be left alone and you should never go anywhere alone (such as to get your diabetes supplies).

granulated sugar; a tablespoon of honey; three or four glucose tablets; or three teaspoons (or three-fourths of a tube) of glucose gel. Not *any* sugary food will do. You want a concentrated sugar that your bloodstream can rapidly absorb. The fat contained in some sweet foods, such as rich pastries or ice cream, will slow the introduction of sugar into the blood.

Once you've eaten the carbohydrate snack, rest for about 20 minutes and then recheck your blood sugar level (it shouldn't be less than 90 mg/dl). Repeat treatment if the blood sugar level still falls below your target range.

Moderate hypoglycemia is treated in the same way but you may need bigger portions of carbs, and it may take longer for you to feel better.

Severe hypoglycemia. Severe hypoglycemia (below 20 mg/dl) rarely occurs and generally can be prevented with prompt treatment when the first signs of low blood sugar are noticed. It occurs when the brain is really starved for fuel (blood sugar), which is why you'll experience severe mental disorientation. In cases of severe hypoglycemia, the school nurse or trained staffers must respond immediately.

If you're experiencing severe symptoms of hypoglycemia, you should never be given anything to eat or drink or have anything put in your mouth, because you could choke. If you have diabetes and lose consciousness or experience convulsions or seizures, you should be placed on your side to prevent choking. A school nurse or other trained person should then administer a glucagon injection, if indicated in your Diabetes Medical Management Plan. While the glucagon is being administered, another person should call for emergency medical assistance. Glucagon is a hormone that raises

Don't Over-Treat!

Eating too *much* sugar in the wake of a low blood sugar episode can cause the opposite problem and make your blood sugar levels soar. No matter how tempting, don't stuff lots of sweets when your blood sugar gets low. Just follow your doctor's advice.

Symptoms of Severe Hypoglycemia

- inability to swallow
- seizures or jerking movements
- unconsciousness
- unresponsiveness
- coma

blood sugar levels by triggering the release of glycogen (stored carbohydrate) from the liver. Although glucagon may cause nausea and vomiting once you regain consciousness, it's a lifesaving treatment.

If glucagon isn't authorized, 911 must be called immediately. A person with severe hypoglycemia needs urgent medical care to restore normal blood sugar levels and stabilize insulin levels. This may require hospitalization.

HYPERGLYCEMIA

At times, blood sugar levels can get too high. This is a condition known as hyperglycemia. High blood sugar levels can happen if you forget to take your medicine on time, if you eat too much or too much of the wrong food, or if you don't get enough exercise. If you get sick, this also can raise your blood sugar levels. Over time, hyperglycemia can lead to serious health problems and damage your eyes, kidneys, nerves, and blood vessels. Hyperglycemia, also called high blood glucose or high blood sugar, is a serious condition in people with diabetes, which may be caused by too little insulin or illness, infection, injury, stress, emotional upset, or eating too much food that hasn't been balanced by the right amount of insulin, or by a drop in activity.

Symptoms. Symptoms of high levels of blood sugar include increased thirst, frequent urination, nausea, blurry vision, and fatigue. Over a long period of time, even moderately high blood sugar levels can lead to serious complications, such as heart disease, blindness, kidney failure, and amputations. In the short term, hyperglycemia can impair your ability to think clearly and lead to poor school performance.

Treating hyperglycemia. If your blood sugar level gets too high, you may need to drink extra water or diet drinks or administer supplemental insulin as directed by your doctor in your Diabetes Medical Management Plan. You should monitor your blood sugar level closely until it returns to the target range as outlined in your DMMP.

DIABETIC KETOACIDOSIS

Hyperglycemia doesn't usually cause short-term problems, but in people with Type 1 diabetes blood sugar levels above 250 mg/dl may cause a life-threatening emergency complication known as diabetic ketoacidosis.

If you don't take your insulin, if a pump malfunctions and delivers less insulin, or if either physical or emotional stress diminishes the effectiveness of your insulin, the body will break down your body fat for energy, causing ketones to form. Ketones are chemicals produced when your body metabolizes fat to provide energy. As ketones build up in your blood, your kidneys clear them out into your urine. But if there are more ketones than the kidneys can handle, they will build up in the blood and may result in diabetic ketoacidosis (DKA).

Symptoms. The first symptoms are excessive urination and thirst with a very high blood sugar reading. One type of ketone (acetone) is expelled through the lungs, giving the breath a characteristic fruity odor. This complication also causes nausea, vomiting, and stomach pain. If untreated, DKA can lead to shortness of breath ("air hunger") and increasing sleepiness. People who use insulin pumps can go into DKA within hours if their pumps stop delivering insulin appropriately.

Diagnosis. At the very first signs of hyperglycemia, you can check your urine for ketones by dipping a special strip into your urine and comparing the resulting color to a color chart. High levels of urinary ketones mean you need to treat your hyperglycemia right away, because ketones that build up in the body for a long time lead to serious illness and coma.

Treating DKA. Treat this problem by administering insulin and drinking plenty of fluids. In severe cases, intravenous feeding may be necessary and you may need to be hospitalized.

Prevention. DKA can be prevented if you check your urine for ketones during times of illness (especially if you're vomiting) or whenever your blood sugar level gets too high.

MEDICAL IDENTIFICATION

It may not look like the latest fashion from Tiffany's, but wearing a medical emergency bracelet or necklace can be critically important in a medical emergency. These alert bracelets are especially important for activities outside of school, where other people might not know you have diabetes. If your blood sugar plummeted and you became unconscious—but no one knew you had diabetes—you might not receive the right treatment quickly enough.

In the old days, there was only one basic style, and it wasn't the most stylish bit of jewelry on the market. Today, there are lots of options, including beaded bracelets, sporty wristbands, watches, and even ankle bracelets! No matter what type of bracelet or wristband you choose, you should wear it on the left, where emergency personnel take your pulse, so they'll see the emergency band right away. If you're self-conscious about wearing medical information jewelry, you can wear a necklace under your shirt or you can carry a "healthkey." This is a special "key" for your keychain that doubles as a medical ID repository of all your health care information, which can be plugged into the USB port of almost any computer manufactured in the past four years.

MedicAlert® Foundation

The MedicAlert® Foundation is a nonprofit health care information organization founded in 1956 that provides medical ID bracelets, key chains, necklaces, and other emergency medical help for a membership fee. Their contact address is: 2323 Colorado Avenue, Turlock, CA 95382; (888) 633-4298; http://www.medicalert.org.

MANAGING YOUR DIABETES AT YOUR FRIEND'S HOUSE

One of the problems that teens experience when they're first diagnosed with diabetes is what to do about visits at friends' homes, especially overnight. Some parents may not embrace the responsibility of caring for someone with diabetes. This is where your parents can help.

If you spend a lot of time at your best friend's house, his or her parents should know the signs of hypoglycemia and how to treat it. It also will be helpful to share your meal plan with them, so they know when it's a good time to offer a snack or a meal. Have your parents talk to them and explain the situation. If you're already testing and giving yourself your own injections, there's little they'll need to do. It may help if your parents make sure to offer to be available by cell phone around the clock during the time you're visiting.

HANDLING DIABETES ON A TRIP

Even if you have diabetes, there's nothing stopping you from hiking a mountain, going on vacation, enjoying a cruise, or traveling across country. You'll just need to do some advance planning, especially if you'll be crossing time zones, eating exotic food, or being more or less active than usual. If this happens, talk to your parents and doctor about diabetes and how it could be handled at a social event or on a trip.

Before you go. Be sure to visit your diabetes specialist to make sure your condition is under control before you leave. If you need any vaccinations, get them at least a month before you depart, so that if the shots make you sick you'll have time to recover before your trip.

If you take insulin and you'll be flying across time zones, bring your flight schedule and information on time zone changes to the doctor's office, so that your doctor or educator can help you plan the timing of your injections while you travel. Remember that if you're flying east, you'll have a shorter day, so if you inject insulin you may not need so much. Going west gives you a longer day, so more insulin may be needed. As you can imagine, this can get confusing. To keep track of shots and meals through changing time zones, keep your watch on your home time zone until the morning after you arrive.

While you're at the doctor's office, get a letter explaining your treatment and listing your diabetes supplies (including insulin, syringes, and any other medications or devices you use). This letter

"I Have Diabetes" around the World

Dutch: Ik heb diabetes. (I have diabetes.)
Suiker of oranje sap, tevreden! (Sugar or orange juice, please!)

French: J'ai le diabète.
Sucre ou jus d'orange, s'il vous plait!

German: Ich habe Diabetes.
Zucker oder Orangensaft, bitte!

Italian: Ho diabete.
Zucchero o succo di arancia, per favore!

Portuguese: Eu tenho o diabetes.
Açúcar ou suco alaranjado, por favor!

Spanish: Tengo diabetes.
Azúcar o jugo anaranjado, por favor!

also should list any allergies you have or any foods or medications to which you are sensitive. In addition, be sure to get a prescription for your insulin or your oral diabetes medication. Of course, you should bring more than enough insulin, syringes, or pills to last through the trip, but the prescription may help in case of emergency.

If you're going to be flying, have your parents request a special meal that's low in sugar, fat, or cholesterol at least two days before the flight. And no matter where you go, you should be sure to wear your medical ID bracelet or necklace that shows you have diabetes.

If you're traveling abroad. There's certainly no reason why people with diabetes can't travel in other countries. If you're going to be traveling beyond the borders of the United States, you can write for a list of International Diabetes Federation groups to: IDF, Avenue Emile De Mot 19, B-1000, Brussels, Belgium (http://www.idf.org).

Your parents may want to get a list of English-speaking foreign doctors by getting free membership in the International Association for Medical Assistance to Travelers (IAMAT), 417 Center Street, Lewiston,

NY 14092 (http://www.iamat.org). If an emergency occurs while you're traveling and you don't have such a list, you can contact the American Consulate, American Express, or local medical schools for a list of doctors. And while you're at it, you might want to learn how to say "I have diabetes" and "sugar or orange juice, please" in the language or languages of the countries you'll visit.

What to pack. When you're going away on a trip, you should pack at least twice as much medication and blood-testing supplies as you think you're going to need. If you're flying, you should put at least half of these supplies in your carry-on bag. Keep up to date on the news and safety requirements as well. This way you know that at least some of your medication will always be with you. In your carry-on bag, you should separate your medication and associated supplies into a separate bag and label your medications. Include all the insulin and syringes you'll need, along with blood and urine-testing supplies, extra batteries for your glucose meter, all oral medications, and other medications or medical supplies, such as glucagon, antidiarrhea medication, antibiotic ointment, and antinausea drugs. You also should include your ID and diabetes identity card, a pack of crackers or cheese, along with peanut butter, fruit, a juice box, and some form of sugar (hard candy or glucose tablets) to treat low blood sugar.

If you're driving or hiking. You don't need to keep your insulin refrigerated, but don't store it in the glove compartment or trunk of the car where it's hot. Also keep in mind that backpacks and bike bags can get really hot in the direct sunlight. If you're going to be exposed to the elements, protect your insulin by packing it in a travel pack so it stays cool.

If you're flying. The first thing you need to worry about is getting your injection equipment past the security checks. Notify the screener right away that you have diabetes and that you're carrying your supplies with you. The following diabetes-related supplies and equipment are allowed through the checkpoint once they've been screened:

- insulin and insulin-loaded dispensing products (such as vials or boxes of individual vials, jet injectors, pens, infusers, and preloaded syringes) as long as they're clearly identified and labeled

- unlimited number of unused syringes when accompanied by insulin or other intravenous medication
- glucagon emergency kit, as long as it's clearly labeled
- lancets, blood glucose meters, blood glucose meter test strips, alcohol swabs, meter-testing solutions
- insulin pump and insulin pump supplies (cleaning agents, batteries, plastic tubing, infusion kit, catheter, and needle)
- urine ketone test strips
- used syringes (an unlimited number) when carried in a hard-surfaced disposal container

In order to prevent contamination or damage, you'll be asked at the security checkpoint to handle and repack your own supplies during the visual inspection process. Any medication or supplies that can't be cleared visually must be submitted for X-ray screening. If you refuse, you won't be allowed to carry your medications and related supplies past the checkpoint.

Insulin pump manufacturers say that pumps can safely go through airport security systems, but if you prefer, you can ask for a visual inspection rather than walking through the metal detector. Tell the screener that you can't remove the insulin pump, since it's connected to a catheter inserted under your skin.

Once on board the plane, you'll face some new challenges with eating and taking insulin. If you've done your homework and followed the suggestions above, you've already preordered your in-flight meal two days before takeoff. If you take insulin before eating, wait until you actually see your food coming down the aisle before you take your shot. Otherwise, if you take your insulin and there's a delay, you could end up with low blood sugar. To be on the safe side, it's a good idea to always carry some food with you. That way, if your meal is delayed or your request gets mixed up, you won't be stuck with an empty stomach.

If you inject insulin while you're in the air, you'll need to be careful not to inject air into the insulin bottle. In the pressurized cabin, pressure differences can make it hard to depress the plunger, which can make it hard to measure insulin accurately.

Once you arrive. Check your blood sugar as soon as possible after you land, because jet lag can make it harder to realize you have low blood sugar. If you've just completed a long flight, take it easy! Don't plan on climbing Mt. Kilimanjaro as soon as you land. Relax for a day or so and check your blood sugar a lot. If you take insulin, plan your activities so you can work in your insulin and meals. If you're more active than usual, your blood sugar could drop, so take along snacks when you're out hiking or sightseeing. Don't assume you'll be able to find food wherever you are.

Remember that as someone with diabetes, you need to be especially careful about keeping your feet protected. Be sure to wear comfortable shoes and never go barefoot. Check your feet every day, looking for blisters, cuts, redness, swelling, and scratches. See a doctor as soon as you notice any infection or inflammation.

TESTS YOUR DOCTOR MAY ORDER

There are two blood tests that your doctor may order from time to time to follow your condition: a hemoglobin A1c and a fructosamine test. Both fructosamine and A1c tests help your doctor monitor your blood sugar, but the A1c test is much more popular and more widely accepted. However, the American Diabetes Association recognizes both tests and says that fructosamine may be useful in situations where the A1c can't be reliably measured.

The A1c test can be used by your doctor to help in treatment decisions when you're first diagnosed; the doctor then may order it two to four times each year. In this test, a blood sample will be drawn from a vein in your arm or from a finger stick. It's then used to calculate the average amount of sugar in your blood over the last two to three months by measuring the concentration of glycosylated hemoglobin. Sugar molecules normally tend to stick to hemoglobin in your red blood cells, and "glycosylated hemoglobin" is a fancy term for hemoglobin that's saturated with sugar. This bound form of sugar and hemoglobin is called A1c (or hemoglobin A1c or glycohemoglobin). The more sugar you have in your blood, the more binds to hemoglobin. By testing the amount of saturated hemoglobin every couple of months, you can tell the average blood sugar level of the preceding eight to 12 weeks. The results are recorded as a percentage (on a scale from 4 to 13) that is linked to your average daily blood sugar level. Therefore, a 10 percent reading would indicate an average daily blood sugar level of 250 mg/dl—which would be worrisome. Anything over 8 percent is considered high; if you have diabetes, a score below 7 percent is excellent. (In nondiabetics, a reading would be about 5 percent.)

Although not as widely used, the fructosamine test may be ordered by your doctor if he or she wants to monitor your average blood sugar over the past two or three weeks, not months. This test also looks for sugar saturation, but of other proteins in the blood, not hemoglobin. This test is usually ordered when a diabetic treatment plan is being started or changed as a way of tracking the effects of the change in diet or medication. Fructosamine levels also may be ordered if you get sick enough so that your insulin requirements change.

In general, the higher the fructosamine concentration, the higher the average blood sugar level in the previous couple of weeks. Trends may be more important than specific values here, so if you notice a trend from a normal to high fructosamine, it may indicate that your blood sugar control isn't good enough. You're getting too much sugar, too little insulin, or your insulin treatment has become less effective. A trend from high to normal fructosamine levels may mean that your treatment regimen changes are working.

Fructosamine may be a better monitoring choice than A1c in a few cases, such as when there are rapid changes in diabetes treatment (fructosamine allows for diet or medication adjustments to be evaluated after a couple of weeks rather than months). That's why fructosamine tests may be ordered along with blood sugar levels to help monitor shifting insulin requirements. A fructosamine test also may be ordered if you have a condition that affects the average age of red blood cells, such as hemolytic anemia or blood loss. In these cases, fructosamine can be used to monitor blood sugar control. However, keep in mind that it may not be possible to tell the difference between the fructosamine concentrations of well-controlled diabetics and nondiabetics, which is why the fructosamine test is not used as a screening tool to identify diabetes.

WHAT YOU NEED TO KNOW

- Food makes blood sugar rise, and exercise and insulin make blood sugar levels drop. With good control of blood sugar, you can lessen or avoid complications.
- A diabetes specialist can help you develop a personal diabetes plan and discuss ways to manage low blood sugar (hypoglycemia) and high blood sugar (hyperglycemia).
- The plan shows you how to eat healthfully, get regular physical activity, check your blood sugar levels, and take insulin or oral medication as prescribed.
- Check your blood sugar levels regularly with a blood glucose meter.
- Diet, activity, insulin, and hormonal changes can affect blood sugar. To control diabetes and prevent complications, blood sugar levels must be as close to normal as possible.

- Check your blood sugar level by pricking the skin and placing a drop of blood on a special test strip, which is then inserted in a glucose meter.
- Blood sugar is usually checked before eating snacks or lunch, before physical activity, or during symptoms of high or low blood sugar.
- Low blood sugar causes hypoglycemia, which can be life threatening, because your brain needs a constant supply of blood sugar to function.
- Hypoglycemia can be caused by taking too much insulin, using fast-acting insulin, forgetting or delaying a meal or snack, not eating enough, exercising too much or too long, drinking alcohol, or recovering from a serious illness or surgery.
- Symptoms of hypoglycemia include shakiness, rapid heartbeat, sudden sweating, feeling cold, anxiety, hunger, blurry vision, concentration problems, confusion, disorientation, dizziness, headache, irritability, lethargy, pallor, personality changes, sleepiness, uncoordination, weakness, or slurred speech.
- Treat hypoglycemia by consuming a low-fat, quick-acting sugar product with 15 grams of carbohydrate, such as four ounces of fruit juice, half a can of *non-diet* soda, or four packets of granulated sugar.
- Symptoms of severe hypoglycemia include inability to swallow, seizures, convulsions, unconsciousness, unresponsiveness, and coma.
- A person experiencing severe hypoglycemia should never be given anything to eat or drink or have anything put in the mouth. A trained person should inject glucagon if indicated while another person calls 911.
- High blood sugar (hyperglycemia) can occur if you forget to take your medicine on time, if you eat too much or too much of the wrong food, if you don't get enough exercise, or you get sick. Over time, hyperglycemia can damage your eyes, kidneys, nerves, and blood vessels.
- During hyperglycemia, you may need to drink extra water or diet drink or administer supplemental insulin as directed by your doctor.

4

Lifestyle and Diabetes

When Ashley was a child, she and her mom were able to manage her Type 1 diabetes pretty well, but as she got older, it seemed to get harder and harder to keep things on an even keel. She shot up three inches in height, seemed to be hungry all the time, and often felt snappy, irritable, and glum as her hormones rose and fell erratically. At the same time, she became more uncomfortable about having to take insulin during school hours and began resisting the strict diet she had always faithfully followed.

There's no doubt about it—adolescence is rough for any kid, but for teens with diabetes it can be even more difficult. You probably know all about the physical and hormonal changes your body goes through as you grow up. What you may not have realized is that those same hormones responsible for changing your body and making your face break out also make it more challenging to manage your diabetes. As your hormone levels fluctuate, your blood sugar may spike or plummet unpredictably.

Puberty can affect your health, and so can specific lifestyle choices you may be considering, such as whether to smoke, drink, take illegal drugs, go on a date, have sex, or get pregnant. Probably every kid you know is dealing with these questions and making decisions about dating, driving, and alcohol. But having diabetes will complicate the choices you make. You need to know as much as you can about how your lifestyle affects your health, so that you can make the best choices for you. This book won't tell you how to live your life, but it will give you important information and show you the consequences of your choices and how they may affect your diabetes so that you can make the best-informed decisions possible.

EMOTIONAL ISSUES

Teens with diabetes typically find it pretty tiresome to take insulin, check blood sugar, follow a meal plan, and carefully regulate exercise. Just when you reach the point in your life when you're becoming more independent, it seems as if you're spending all this time tending to your health care. Without question, diabetes can make the normal problems of being a teen even more difficult. That's why it's normal, if not healthy, for teens with diabetes to ease up on their diabetes care and try to act like everyone else. And just when your life gets busier and more complicated than ever, your diabetes treatment plan often becomes more challenging. Your changing hormones may make it seem as if you have to readjust your diabetes treatment every other week! As your hormonal levels rise, you may find yourself feeling more moody or irritable. In fact, you may have to check your blood sugar more often to help you distinguish between a normal bad mood and low blood sugar (hypoglycemia). You may feel down a lot, angry, or more stressed about having diabetes than usual. The good news about adolescence is that all this emotional craziness doesn't last forever.

You may feel a lot of conflicting emotions during this period of your life. You may feel like pretending that you don't have diabetes, or you may try to get out of taking shots. Maybe you "forget" to take your insulin sometimes, neglect to check your blood sugar, or start pigging out on pizza and fries. You may try not to think about diabetes for as long as possible. Sometimes you may feel angry and wonder: Why am I the one with diabetes? You might resent your parents, your friends, or your brothers and sisters who don't have diabetes. Of course, what you're really angry at is the diabetes itself. At other times, you may just feel sad, tired, or hopeless. Some of this is normal teenage angst. After all, you've got a serious condition, so a little sadness is quite normal. Some teens worry about their diabetes and feel phobic about needles or constantly worry about having a hypoglycemic reaction. Others might feel guilt because they think their illness is causing hassles for the rest of the family.

Try to remember that it's totally normal to experience uncomfortable emotions of anger, sadness, and confusion, either singly or all at the same time. That doesn't mean you have to drift alone with these feelings, though, especially if they are bothering you a great deal and interfering with the way you want to live your life.

What you can do. Talk to your parents or siblings about how you're feeling, or share some of your thoughts with close friends. You'll be amazed at how much better simply talking about a problem can make you feel.

When you're feeling angry, tense, keyed up, or stressed, do something active, like shooting some hoops, rollerblading, or riding your bike.

If you're feeling introspective, try writing out all your feelings in a journal or a notebook. Write a story or a poem about how you feel. Lots of kids these days are turning to online journals and Web sites such as MySpace, Livejournal, Xanga, or Facebook. These Internet sites have the added bonus of being interactive; if you choose, some of your closest friends can visit your site and make comments and see how you're feeling. Because you can design these Web sites with photos and art and your favorite music, many teens find that putting down their feelings online is a helpful creative outlet.

If you don't want to write down your feelings and you're feeling too stressed to concentrate, try some relaxation exercises, such as yoga, deep breathing, meditation, or tensing and relaxing one muscle at a time. Take some deep breaths, count to 10, and visualize a calm, peaceful spot.

Sometimes it helps to do something to take the focus off your diabetes, even if it's just for a few brief times at first. Call up some friends and suggest that you all do something fun—like go out and watch a movie, rent a video, or go to the mall.

Some kids have found that joining a self-help group or going to diabetes camp (http://www.childrenwithdiabetes.com/camps) with other teens with diabetes can be really helpful. Just seeing that there are lots of other kids in your situation is an amazing feeling; you can share your experiences with kids who really know exactly what it's like.

Find a Support Group

If you or your parents are interested in getting involved with a diabetes group, you can ask your doctor or diabetes educator for a referral. Or, just call 1-800-DIABETES to find out where the closest diabetes support groups are located in your area.

If sad feelings don't go away. Feelings of sadness and loss are a normal reaction to the diagnosis of diabetes, but some people with this condition can become more seriously depressed. In fact, some studies have suggested that clinical depression is about three times more common in people with diabetes than in the healthy population.

Signs of depression include:

- remitting sadness
- loss of interest in things you used to enjoy
- sleeping problems (too much or too little)
- eating problems (eating too much or not enough)
- losing or gaining lots of extra weight
- concentration problems
- tiredness
- anxiety
- frequent crying
- suicidal thoughts

If you feel that you've got some persistent sad or depressed feelings, ask your parents for a referral for some short-term mental health counseling. Sometimes talking to someone not in your family or among your friends can provide a new perspective. Unfortunately, not every adult is open to the idea of mental health counseling, so if you feel the need to speak to someone other than your parents, turn to a trusted teacher, guidance counselor, principal, religious leader, or even an unrelated adult friend. If you're 18, you can refer yourself.

You might want to visit your doctor first, to rule out any physical cause of the depression. A mental health professional can offer you therapy and may prescribe medication for depression as well. There are many different types of psychotherapy, but modern methods of treating depression usually work at either changing your behavior with behavioral therapy or changing your thoughts and your behavior at the same time (a type of counseling called cognitive-behavioral therapy).

Nothing scary or weird will happen during therapy. In a typical treatment plan, you'll meet with a therapist each week for about three months to talk about your diabetes or any events or feelings that trouble you. With the mental health care expert, you'll learn how to handle your depression by eliminating your ideas, fears, or behaviors that reinforce your depression. Sometimes you might work in a group of teens with similar problems.

For example, Susan was getting ready to start a new high school, and she was feeling very uncomfortable about how the other kids were going to treat her. What if they thought she was a freak? What if she had a hypoglycemic episode right in the middle of algebra? How was she going to manage the cafeteria and would she find enough time to inject her insulin? The more she worried, the bigger deal her diabetes seemed to be. Soon, she was worried that every kid in school was staring at her and thinking she was odd, almost as if she was walking around with a big red "D" on her forehead.

The reality, of course, was not like she imagined it. Although diabetes loomed large in *her* universe, the other kids didn't think twice about it. But on her own, Susan was in no shape to recognize this. With the help of a talented cognitive behavioral therapist, she was able to recognize her unhelpful thought patterns. When she caught herself walking down the hall thinking, I'm the only kid in the world with a problem, and everyone is staring at me because I know I look different somehow, she was able to "catch" this thought and stop her spiraling worries. Is that kid looking at me? she challenged herself. No. No one is looking at me. I'm fine.

Her therapist taught her positive ways to think about herself and the other students and encouraged her to try out for the school play and to learn how to relax when she started getting tense. Eventually, Susan was able to realize that although diabetes was a huge deal to her, it didn't faze the other kids at all except for some extra sympathy and a few friendly winces when they heard she had to take daily insulin injections.

As you get older, you'll continue to face new challenges as you take on more responsibility for your own care. You'll have to deal with changes in diabetes treatments and adapt to handling diabetes in high school, summer camp, and college. Remember that at any time you feel overwhelmed, a brief consultation with a mental health specialist can help put things in perspective and keep you on track.

A WORD TO GIRLS

If you're a teenage girl, you have some special issues with diabetes. You may find that your menstrual cycle affects your diabetes, especially during the last half of your cycle. You'll have special concerns about pregnancy (more about this later), and you'll be at higher risk for developing eating disorders and heart disease than women without diabetes.

Many girls and women with diabetes notice than when their period arrives, no matter how careful they are their blood sugar levels spike. This happens because the female hormones estrogen and progesterone both interfere with the action of insulin. The higher the level of these hormones, the more likely you're going to be insulin resistant, and the higher your blood sugar will rise, whether you have Type 1 or Type 2 diabetes. So whether you're injecting insulin or simply managing your diabetes with oral medications, diet, or exercise, your hormone status will affect your blood sugar.

You'll likely have the most trouble during the last half of your 28-day cycle. The release of the egg from the ovary (ovulation) occurs about the 14th day; over the next two weeks, the levels of estrogen and progesterone rise. Right before you get your period, your hormone levels peak, and this is the moment when insulin resistance is strongest and blood sugar levels are highest. At this point in the month, you may discover that your typical treatment plan isn't enough to control your blood sugar.

In order to keep control of your blood sugar, start by trying to figure out exactly when you ovulate, since that marks the moment when your hormone levels start to rise. To do this you can take your temperature with a special "ovulation thermometer" or you can test your urine with an ovulation predictor kit (which costs more, but is more accurate). If you keep a record of your blood sugar readings on arising each morning, after a few months you should be able to predict the monthly changes in your blood sugar levels. Typically, these should be fairly constant and measurable from one month to the next.

By charting these changes, you'll be able to predict when your blood sugar will start to rise each month so that you can get more exercise, change your diet, or—with your doctor's okay—change your medication. If you're injecting insulin, you could slowly increase the dose of longer-acting insulin to boost blood levels of insulin right before your period. If you're using an insulin pump, you may need to adjust the basal rate.

PMS and diabetes. Even if you're not measuring your temperature or your urine, you may be able to figure out your hormone peaks right before your period by your mood alone. If you feel jittery, depressed, irritable, or you retain water and crave certain foods (especially chocolate, carbs, and fat), you may have premenstrual syndrome (PMS). This typically occurs when the levels of progesterone are very high. The problem with food cravings at this time of the month in girls with diabetes is that you typically crave foods that can disrupt your blood sugar levels.

Girls and women with PMS have found a number of ways to ease their symptoms without resorting to endless snacking. First, try to avoid certain foods that only make symptoms worse, including alcohol, chocolate, caffeine, and salty foods. Get lots of exercise, plenty of rest, and practice relaxation techniques such as deep breathing, meditation, and yoga. If none of these measures work, talk to your doctor about prescribing medication to ease PMS symptoms.

DRIVING AND DIABETES

If you're not yet 16, you're probably counting down the days until you hit the magic number so you can get your learner's permit. You'll be happy to hear that even if you do have diabetes, you should have no problem getting a license in most states, as long as you can pass your driving test and you aren't limited by certain complications of diabetes. But because of the danger of driving with low blood sugar, you may be required to submit a written report from your doctor confirming that your diabetes is in relatively good control.

All states do have special licensing rules governing medical conditions that may apply to people with diabetes. Some states apply these rules to all drivers with diabetes, while others apply them only to those who have actually experienced episodes of altered consciousness as a result of the disease or who have other complications of diabetes. Some of these special licensing rules may require you to get a periodic medical exam or prohibit you from driving for a period of time after an episode in which you've lost consciousness.

Once you get your license. Now that you've got that valuable piece of paper in your hand, you'll just want to keep a few common-sense rules in mind. First, you should wear some form of medical identification (a bracelet or necklace) to let others know that you have diabetes and use insulin. This could save your life if you have an accident and you're unconscious. The medical rescue team will alert others that you have diabetes and may need sugar or insulin.

Remember that insulin and some oral medications can make your blood sugar too high or too low, so that at times you may feel sleepy, dizzy, or confused, or you may experience blurred vision,

Specific State Driving Laws

To see specific laws for each state, visit the American Diabetes Association Web site at: http://www.diabetes.org/advocacy-and-legal resources/discrimination/drivers/pvt-licensemap.jsp.

unconsciousness, or a seizure. For this reason, you should always check your blood sugar level before getting in the car, especially before you start on a long trip. Your health care team can help you determine when you should check your blood sugar level before driving and how often you should check while driving.

Make sure you always carry your blood glucose meter and plenty of snacks (such as fruit, juice, crackers, or soda) with you when you drive. Check your blood sugar before you start the car. If your blood sugar is under 80, treat it with 10 to 15 grams of carbohydrate, followed by a snack, and wait until you're at a safer level before starting the ignition. You should never drive when your blood sugar level is too low, because this condition will interfere with your ability to make good choices, to focus on your driving, or to control your car.

Keep your glove compartment stocked with glucose tablets and snacks, so that you're always prepared. If your blood sugar drops while you're driving, pull over as soon as you feel any of the symptoms and check your blood sugar. If your level is low, eat a snack that contains a fast-acting sugar, such as juice, soda with sugar (not diet), hard candy, or glucose tablets. Wait 15 minutes, and then check your blood sugar again. Once your blood sugar level has risen to your target range, you can eat a more substantial snack or meal containing protein. Don't continue driving until your blood sugar level has improved. Always carry a cell phone so you can call for help if you have an emergency while driving alone.

Most people with diabetes experience warning signs of a low blood sugar level, but not everyone does. If you're one of those people who don't notice, you should be especially careful to check before getting behind the wheel. However, if your blood sugar levels drop suddenly for no reason and without advance warning, you shouldn't drive. Discuss with your health care team about whether glycemic awareness training might help you sense the beginning stages of hypoglycemia, what range of blood sugar levels are safe for driving, and if and how often you should pull over and check during a car trip.

Driving Tip

Don't leave blood glucose meters, test strips, or insulin in the car, because temperature fluctuations can damage them.

Find a Driving Specialist

To find a driving specialist near you, contact the Association of Driver Rehabilitation Specialists (800-290-2344) or visit their Web site at: http://www.aded.net.

In the long run, diabetes can lead to problems that may affect driving, such as nerve damage in your hands, legs, feet, or eyes. If you're having complications of diabetes such as vision or sensation problems, your diabetes health care team can refer you to a driving specialist who can give you on- and off-road tests to see whether your diabetes is impairing your driving. You can also schedule extra training with this specialist to improve your driving skills. Alternatively, you may prefer to work with an occupational therapist, who can help with the driving skills assessment.

DATING

It's probably no secret among your close friends that you have diabetes, and if they're good friends, your condition most likely doesn't affect the way they treat you. You can even count on them to help treat your low blood sugar if it ever came to that. But once you're old enough to start thinking about dating, you may realize this opens up entire new areas you're going to have to deal with.

The fact that you have diabetes may not be widely known at your school, and whom you choose to share your medical history with is certainly your choice. Telling your close friends is one thing—telling a boyfriend or girlfriend may be quite another. Most kids who have diabetes say that they've found it's best to start out simple and direct with something like: "I'd like to tell you something . . ." Then explain that you just want her (or him) to know that you're healthy, you're taking medication, and diabetes isn't contagious. Most teens believe that if a girlfriend or boyfriend is going to be spending time with you, especially if you'll be alone together, the person should know some of the warning signs in case your blood sugar gets low.

Many kids decide that it's simply easier to tell a date about the diabetes ahead of time so they don't have to worry about dealing with the issue in the middle of the date. But if you've recently met and you don't know the person really well or this is a first date, it may seem awkward to suddenly bring up a health problem.

Think through what you'll be doing on the date to see whether it makes sense to discuss your diabetes before you go out. If it's just a quick movie, you may choose not to bring up the subject. But if you'll be having a meal, will it be awkward if your date wants you to eat a big, gooey dessert? Will you be able to follow your meal plan at the restaurant? Will you need a snack at some point in the evening? Will it be easier to stick to your meal plan if your date knows about your diabetes?

You'll also need to figure out how long the date will last, so you'll know whether you'll have to check your blood sugar or take insulin while you're out. Will this be a fairly quiet evening watching a play or listening to music? Or will you be dancing or ice skating all night, which will require extra checks, some snacks, or a risk of low blood sugar?

SEX AND PREGNANCY

Teens with diabetes struggle with the same issues about having sex as do teens without diabetes. It's just that having diabetes adds an extra dimension to the possible consequences of being sexually active. If you're a woman, it's important for you to understand that diabetes doesn't make it any harder for you to get pregnant, but it *does* increase the risks associated with pregnancy.

During adolescence, your blood sugar is typically harder to keep in the target range, and you probably are recording lots more high levels than normal. High blood sugar can cause birth defects in an unborn baby. This doesn't mean you can't plan to get pregnant when you're older and more prepared for a baby. When you're ready to have a child, a woman with diabetes must plan her pregnancies carefully, making sure that her blood sugar level is extremely well controlled right from the start.

If you're thinking you might want to engage in sex, you need to take responsibility for that decision and plan ahead. Don't rely on your partner to handle this crucial task. It's your body and your responsibility to keep yourself safe. Talk to your doctor about birth control, learn all you can, and never have unprotected sex.

ALCOHOL AND DIABETES

You should already know about the dangers of drinking too much and of drinking and driving. For people with diabetes, however, even a little alcohol can be dangerous. Alcohol alone lowers blood sugar levels, but the sugary mixers in some drinks can raise blood sugar. Yet as you drink, the alcohol clouds your brain and makes it difficult to recognize the signs of low blood sugar. You may think that you're feeling the effects of alcohol, when in fact your blood sugar is plummeting. Your friends may misunderstand your erratic behavior and assume you're drunk, even if they know you have diabetes. In addition, heavy drinking over time can damage your liver so that it won't be able to produce sugar as well. When this happens, your diabetes will become harder to control.

How alcohol affects you. Alcohol moves very quickly into the blood without being broken down in your stomach; in fact, within five minutes of having an alcoholic drink, there's enough alcohol in your blood that it can be measured. Between 30 to 90 minutes after having a drink, the alcohol in your bloodstream peaks.

It's your liver's job to break down the alcohol once it's in your body, but that takes time. If you weigh 150 pounds, it will take about two hours to break down the alcohol in just one beer or mixed drink. If you drink alcohol faster than your liver can break it down—more than one drink every two hours—the excess alcohol moves through your bloodstream to other parts of your body. Brain cells are easy targets. When someone talks about feeling a "buzz" from alcohol, the effect on brain cells is what they're talking about.

If you have diabetes and take insulin shots or diabetes pills, you run the risk of developing low blood sugar when you drink alcohol. This is why you should never drink on an empty stomach. Alcohol increases the risk of having low blood sugar because of your liver. Normally, when your blood sugar level starts to drop, your liver steps in to change stored carbohydrates into glucose (sugar). Then it sends the sugar into the blood, in order to slow down a low blood sugar reaction. This all changes when alcohol enters the system. Never forget that your body reacts to alcohol as if it is a poison, and your liver wants to get it out of the blood as quickly as possible. In fact, the liver won't produce sugar again until it has dealt with this pesky alcohol problem. Therefore, if your blood sugar level is falling and you're drinking alcohol, you can quickly wind up with very low blood sugar. This is why drinking as little as two drinks on an empty stomach can lead to very low blood sugar.

If you mix alcohol and exercise, you also increase the risk of low blood sugar. Remember that exercise alone helps lower your blood sugar levels. For example, if you've just played a few tough sets of tennis on a hot day and your friends break out the beer to celebrate after the match, you're no longer exercising, but your body is busy replacing the energy your muscles used up by removing sugar from the blood and adding it to your muscles. This is why exercise makes your blood sugar level drop. If you take insulin or diabetes pills, they too are working to remove sugar from your blood. So unless you eat or your liver adds sugar to your blood, you could be heading for a low blood sugar level. If you then drink a beer, the alcohol stops your liver from producing sugar because it's busy dealing with the alcohol. Your chance of having low blood sugar levels is even greater.

Low blood sugar when drinking is less of a risk for those with Type 2 diabetes, who control their diabetes with meal planning and exercise alone. But it's still a risk. And if you take oral diabetes medication for your Type 2 diabetes, you'll need to check with your health care provider to see if it's okay to combine alcohol with your medications. And remember that although an occasional drink may not hurt your blood sugar control, it can interfere with your eating plan if your goal is weight loss. Two light beers equal about 200 extra calories, and those are "empty" calories, because they don't provide any nutrients. If you're following a low-calorie meal plan, you may want to avoid alcohol. In general, alcohol counts as a fat serving (one drink equals two fat exchanges).

Total abstinence. While alcohol isn't good for anybody with diabetes, some people with diabetes really should not drink any alcohol at all. Alcohol can worsen some diabetic complications such as damage to the nerves in your arms or legs. Alcohol is toxic to nerves, so drinking can increase the pain, burning, tingling, numbness, and other symptoms. In fact, some studies have found that even drinking less than two drinks a week can trigger nerve damage.

Taking a Sobriety Test

Some of the signs of being drunk–such as confusion or slurred speech–are a lot like the effects of a low blood sugar reaction or ketoacidosis (most common in people with Type 1 diabetes who haven't taken enough insulin). If you haven't been drinking but you're asked to take a blood or a breath test for alcohol because of these signs, don't worry. Diabetes won't affect the results of a test for alcohol, even if you're having a reaction or have a fruity smell to your breath because of high ketone levels. If you are asked to take a test for alcohol and you have a choice, choose a blood test, because that way health care providers can check your levels of sugar and ketones too.

Heavy drinking (three or more drinks a day) may worsen diabetes-related eye disease. And if you have high blood pressure, you can lower it if you stop drinking alcohol. Those who have diabetes and who also have high levels of triglycerides in their blood should not drink alcohol, because alcohol affects how the liver clears fat from the blood. Alcohol also encourages the liver to make more triglycerides, which is the last thing you need. Even light drinking of only two four-ounce glasses of wine a week can boost triglyceride levels.

How to say no. In most states, drinking is illegal until you're 18 or 21, but despite this, many teens drink anyway. Even if you're aware of the problem of mixing alcohol and diabetes and you'd rather not drink, it can be hard sometimes to say no when all your friends are drinking. One way to sidestep this problem is to serve as your friends' "designated driver." This is usually a well-accepted excuse not to drink and will be a decision that's respected by most teens. Another way is to have a beverage that looks like an alcohol-containing cocktail, but isn't. Try a "virgin" Bloody Mary or piña colada without alcohol. Looks great, tastes great, but it's alcohol free.

Drink as safely as you can. If you do decide that you want to drink, there are ways to drink that are safer than others for people with diabetes. First of all, remember that the American Diabetes Association suggests that you have no more than two drinks a day if you are a man and no more than one drink a day if you are a woman. (This recommendation is the same for people without diabetes.)

Next, you should never drink on an empty stomach, because this will almost assuredly trigger a drop in blood sugar. But don't assume that a few handfuls of salted peanuts from the snack bowl will offset that hypoglycemia; those bar snacks are usually loaded with salt and far too fatty. Instead, before you go out for the evening, eat something healthy from your diabetes meal plan.

If you're determined to drink, you should learn the alcohol and carbohydrate content of various drinks so you can choose the ones with lower alcohol and sugar. Remember that some alcoholic drinks are better choices for people with diabetes than others. If you use mixers in your drinks, choose ones that are sugar free, such as diet soft drinks, diet tonic, club soda, seltzer, or water. This will help keep your blood sugar levels in your target range. Light beer and dry wines are better choices than their full-strength cousins because they have less alcohol and carbohydrates and fewer calories. To dilute the alcohol and make a drink last longer, try a spritzer. Mix wine with sparkling water, club soda, or diet soda.

Warning

Glucagon shots don't help severe low blood sugar caused by drinking. Glucagon shots treat very severe low blood sugar reactions caused by too much insulin. They work by prompting your liver to release more sugar into your blood, but alcohol stops this process. You need to be able to treat your reaction with a carbohydrate, such as oral glucose tablets or gels, so you need to avoid letting a low blood sugar level get severe. If you pass out, you'll need to have glucose injected into your bloodstream by a health care professional.

And no matter how low in alcohol or sugar, if you really insist on drinking you should limit yourself to just one or two alcohol beverages and avoid drinks with sugary mixers. And no matter what, if you're going out to drink you should always wear your medical ID.

If you've been drinking, once you get home check your blood sugar before you go to sleep. Eat a snack before you go to bed to avoid a low blood sugar reaction while you sleep.

ILLEGAL DRUGS

In addition to the fact that they're illegal and dangerous, street drugs can cause extra problems for kids with diabetes, much like alcohol. Some illegal drugs lower blood sugar and others raise it; in addition, drug use can mask the symptoms of hypoglycemia. If you're under the influence of drugs, you may not be able to recognize a problem with low blood sugar. And because some drugs (such as marijuana) make you very hungry, you may eat lots of the wrong kinds of food and throw off your blood sugar. Other drugs (such as Ecstasy) can make you feel extremely energetic, prompting you to party all night without resting or eating properly. It's best to avoid illegal drugs—or any drug your doctor hasn't approved for use.

SMOKING AND DIABETES

Smoking and chewing tobacco are dangerous for anyone, causing thousands of lung cancer and heart disease deaths every year. Smoking also can cause or worsen asthma, sinus infections, allergies, and a host of other health problems. For people with diabetes, smoking is even more dangerous. If you have diabetes, you're already at higher risk for developing heart disease and kidney problems, no matter how old you are. Using tobacco on top of that risk is just asking for trouble.

In addition, each time you light up, smoking constricts the blood vessels all through your body. Because diabetes already can cause circulatory problems, you should avoid anything that further constricts your blood vessels already weakened by diabetes.

Some kids assume that chewing tobacco is safer than smoking, because they're not breathing the toxic fumes into the lungs. In fact, chewing tobacco is even worse, because your body absorbs even more nicotine from chewing tobacco than it does from cigarettes. Chewing tobacco and snuff also are linked to mouth and nose cancer.

If you already smoke or chew, quitting can protect you from further damage from tobacco. No matter how long you've been smoking, the minute you quit your body begins to repair the damage the nicotine and other poisons have caused. It's really hard to quit, however, so talk to your doctor about ways to make quitting easier.

EATING DISORDERS AND DIABETES

You probably know how common eating disorders are among teens, especially girls. Maybe some of your friends have an eating disorder. There is some evidence that girls with diabetes (especially Type 1) may be more prone to eating disorders, perhaps because of the enormous attention they must pay to food. Some teenage girls feel uncomfortable about their bodies and perceive themselves as weak, damaged, or out of control because they have diabetes, which leads them to want to control the one area they *can*—their weight. Some teens who have diabetes and who also have an eating disorder learn how to manipulate their diabetes treatment so that they lose weight.

Teens with diabetes and eating disorders may show some or all of the following warning signs:

- unhealthy preoccupation with food and weight
- extreme blood sugar fluctuations
- frequent low blood sugar (hypoglycemia)
- frequent high blood sugar (hyperglycemia)
- talking about losing too much weight
- choosing an extremely low-fat or low-calorie diet
- binge eating
- insulin manipulation

Find an Eating Disorder Specialist

To find a specialist in the treatment of eating disorders, contact the National Eating Disorders Association at (800) 931-2237 or visit their Web site at: http://www.nationaleatingdisorders.org.

Anorexia. Anorexia nervosa is an extreme obsession with food and physical appearance, and people with this disorder literally starve themselves by cutting back on food and exercising excessively. No matter how thin they get—and some girls can become almost skeletal—people with anorexia still see themselves as fat. Anorexic girls who have diabetes may skip an insulin injection, or not use enough, which boosts their blood sugar levels, triggering excess urination and leading to weight loss.

Bulimia. Girls with bulimia are also obsessed with food and being thin, but to reach their goals they eat large amounts of food (binge) only to vomit it all up or take laxatives afterward (purging). Girls with diabetes and bulimia may manipulate their insulin so they don't gain weight. Others may take diuretics (drugs that flush out excess fluid from the body) in an attempt to lose weight. If you have diabetes, you should know that using diuretics can affect your blood sugar and increase the amount of insulin you need.

Although most often people exhibit only one form of eating disorder, it's also possible to have anorexia and bulimia at the same time. In any case, untreated eating disorders can have serious health consequences, and manipulating insulin can cause more problems with diabetes. Any teen with an eating disorder should be treated by a mental health professional with expertise in this area, because these conditions can be life threatening.

WHAT YOU NEED TO KNOW

- As hormone levels fluctuate, your blood sugar may spike or plummet unpredictably.

- It's normal to experience anger, sadness, or confusion about having diabetes, but if depression doesn't go away, you should seek help. Clinical depression is about three times more common in people with diabetes than in the healthy population.
- The menstrual cycle affects diabetes, especially during the last half of the cycle; blood sugar often spikes when your period arrives.
- Teen girls with diabetes have special concerns about pregnancy and are at higher risk for developing eating disorders and heart disease.
- Because of the danger of driving with low blood sugar, to get a license you may have to get your doctor to confirm your diabetes is in relatively good control.
- Always check your blood sugar level before getting in the car, especially before you start on a long trip.
- Pull over if your blood sugar drops while driving, check your blood sugar, and if your level is low eat a fast-acting sugar. Don't continue driving until your blood sugar level has improved.
- Diabetes doesn't make it any harder for you to get pregnant, but it *does* increase the risks associated with pregnancy.
- Even a little alcohol can be dangerous for people with diabetes.
- Alcohol lowers blood sugar levels, but the sugary mixers in some drinks can raise blood sugar. As you drink, it's hard to recognize the signs of low blood sugar.
- If you haven't been drinking but you're asked to take a blood or a breath test for alcohol, diabetes won't affect the results of a test for alcohol, even if you're having a reaction or have a fruity smell to your breath because of high ketone levels.
- If you're asked to take a test for alcohol and you have a choice, choose a blood test, because health care providers can check your levels of sugar and ketones.
- Street drugs can cause problems for teens with diabetes, masking some diabetic symptoms and making it harder to control your health.
- Teens with diabetes are at higher risk for developing heart disease and kidney problems, and smoking only increases the risk.
- There is some evidence that girls with diabetes (especially Type 1) may be more prone to eating disorders.

5

Diabetes at School

Brittany was a bubbly 15-year-old who spent most of her spare time in front of her computer, sending instant messages and e-mail to her friends and designing Web sites with the latest software. She could be found most nights surrounded by bags of cookies and chips, sodas, and cupcakes at her desk, and the only exercise she got was her once-a-week gym class at school. Because she was an excellent student, her family ignored her terrible diet and the extra 30 pounds she put on when she hit puberty, but when her family doctor diagnosed Type 2 diabetes, the whole family was shocked.

Brittany had to control her blood sugar with diet, exercise, and oral medications, and she was apprehensive about going back to school. What would the other kids say? Would the teachers make a big deal out of her condition? What if she got hypoglycemic in gym class? What if a teacher stopped her from snacking as she was supposed to do? Kids who must take insulin injections have even more concerns. It's important to learn everything you need to know about handling your disease while at school.

If you've been diagnosed with diabetes, you've probably already met with a diabetes educator trained to help you handle your diabetes. (A diabetes educator who has passed a test about diabetes care is also called a CDE, for Certified Diabetes Educator.) Your CDE probably asked you a lot of questions about what you do at school and gave you some ideas about how to make good food choices in the cafeteria, what to do in gym class, where to keep snacks in class, and other things. There's a good reason for this: You spend about one-third of your time in school (not counting after-school activities), so you can't ignore your diabetes while you're away from home.

Diabetes medical management plan. Your diabetes educator has probably worked with you and your parents to create a health care plan or a diabetes medical management plan (DMMP), which outlines everything you need to do to manage your diabetes at school. It should include things such as the date you were diagnosed, your current health status, emergency contacts, a list of diabetes equipment and supplies, and specific medical orders for blood sugar testing and medications to be given at school (such as insulin, glucagon, and oral drugs). It also will include a meal and snack plan, exercise requirements, and any other monitoring that is required. The plan should include a description of symptoms of high and low blood sugar and prescribed treatment for these conditions. It should be in place before you go back to school and be updated whenever your status or treatment changes, at the beginning of each school year, and if there are any changes in how you manage your own care.

Your parents should supply the school with a glucagon emergency kit to be administered by trained school personnel in case your blood sugar ever falls seriously low. This kit usually contains a bottle of glucagon in powder form and a prefilled syringe with special liquid; the two are mixed just before a glucagon injection is given. Glucagon may be stored at room temperature. The school nurse and trained diabetes personnel must have access to the glucagon emergency kit at all times.

MEETING WITH THE SCHOOL

Blake's mom sets up a meeting with the teachers, the nurse, and the middle school principal every year before school starts to discuss Blake's Type 1 diabetes. She comes armed with brochures about diabetes, especially how it pertains to Blake. (There are some really good brochures available.) In addition, his mom types out a sheet listing his symptoms of low and high blood sugar and what to do if the symptoms appear. She has also discovered it's a good idea to give a copy of this information to his bus driver.

Before you go back to school, you and your parents should meet with school staff to discuss your diabetes and how you'll take care of it. It's important that the school understands your plan and how it's going to work. Your parents should bring a copy of your DMMP. You and your parents may later make changes to the plan, but having a document to work with will keep the meeting on track. Your diabetes educator can give you some pamphlets or information sheets about diabetes that you can give to school officials or even come to this first meeting with you.

School staffers should work together to follow the details of your DMMP. This way, everyone knows exactly what is expected of them, and what the school's roles and responsibilities are. Based on your DMMP, you, your parents, and the school can prepare an emergency plan that describes how to recognize hypoglycemia and hyperglycemia and what to do as soon as symptoms of either are noticed. You and your parents should meet with your school each year, to review your plan and update it. You'll need to update your plan sooner if you change the way you take care of your diabetes.

What your parents need to do. In general, your parents should provide all diabetes equipment and snacks to the school and take an active role in educating and training school personnel in diabetes care. Your parents also need to make sure the school can reach them at any time in case of emergency. Having them carry a cell phone is probably the best way to handle that.

What the school needs to do. The school nurse is the most appropriate person at your school to help you, but many schools don't have a full-time nurse. Even if your school has a full-time nurse, he or she may not always be available. Since diabetes emergencies can happen at any time, other school personnel should be trained and ready to provide diabetes care for you at school and at all school-sponsored activities in which you participate. Your school nurse or another qualified health professional should help train school staff. Everyone at your school who works with you should receive information about diabetes, how to identify medical emergencies, and whom to contact in case of an emergency.

At least two adults at school should be trained to recognize and treat blood sugar that is too high or too low, how to check for ketones, and what to do if your ketone level is abnormal. If you're old enough to treat yourself, you should be allowed to do this, but your teachers should understand that you need to be supervised at all times during a hypoglycemic reaction. They must make sure you never walk alone to another part of the school to test your blood sugar or to get treatment. It's critically important that you know exactly which school staff members are trained to help you in the event of an emergency.

If you require insulin injections during school hours, two adults at school should be trained to give them or supervise you as you administer your own injection. Two adults also should be trained to give a glucagon injection. The school should provide a location where you can check your blood sugar or take insulin privately (but still with adult supervision, if needed).

At least two adults should be familiar with your meal plan, and they should work with your parents to coordinate it with the daily schedule. The school should also notify you and your parents whenever special events come up that might affect the meal plan.

You and your parents must make sure *all* the people who will interact with you during the day are aware of your condition; this includes bus drivers, cafeteria workers, coaches, school volunteers, field trip chaperones, standardized test monitors, and parents of your friends. *All* adults who are responsible for supervising you at school should be trained to recognize low and high blood sugar and know emergency procedures. It's especially important that anyone who will be with you right before meals, in mid-afternoon, and after exercise understand your condition, since this is when blood sugar levels tend to drop, requiring special attention.

Everyone at school should understand that you must be allowed to see the school nurse whenever you need to. School staff also must allow you to eat a snack anywhere and to use the restroom and drink water at any time. This is important, because high blood sugar levels increase urination and may lead to dehydration if you can't replace the fluids. The school also must give you a safe place to store your insulin and glucagon and allow you immediate access to your diabetes supplies at any time. Your school must make sure you can participate in all sports, extracurricular activities, and field trips with any necessary supervision.

Safe supply disposal. You, your parents, and the school must decide how to dispose of your glucose monitoring supplies. Make sure school staff know that checking your blood sugar levels won't present a danger to other students or workers when there is a plan for proper disposal of lancets and other material that may touch blood. You all should agree on the plan, which should be consistent with standard "universal precautions" for handling of biohazardous materials and local waste disposal laws. The disposal container should be a heavy duty plastic or metal can with a tight-fitting lid.

Telling your class. You or your parents may decide to talk to your class. If you're shy or not much of a public speaker, you could ask your diabetes educator to talk to the class. These professionals are trained to talk about diabetes, and they'll be able to answer any questions your classmates and teachers might have.

On the other hand, you're not *required* to educate the world. You don't need to feel like you have to talk to your class about diabetes, even if your teachers ask you to. Some kids like to speak in front of groups, and others don't. You might feel like you just want to keep details about your diabetes private, and that's perfectly okay too. You can simply answer any questions about diabetes one at a time, if your friends ask you. But how much you tell your classmates or who you talk to about diabetes at school is up to you.

Telling your close friends. When your good friends find out you have diabetes, they'll probably have lots of questions; this is your chance to tell them what you've learned. They may have heard things that aren't true, or they may not understand what diabetes really means. Your parents, doctor, or diabetes educator can help you plan what you're going to say. They may even be able to give you information to pass out.

Some kids don't have any problems in sharing their latest health problem with their good friends. Other kids worry about whether they'll be accepted or thought of as "sick" or "odd." After all, nobody likes to be different. This can be especially difficult during middle school, at a time when wanting to blend in is at an all-time high. But telling your friends about diabetes doesn't have to be a big deal, and the way you handle it can affect how your friends accept the idea. It may only take a few minutes. One of the first things to do is to reassure them that they can't catch it from you! Then you might say something like:

> "Having diabetes just means that I have to be careful to eat at certain times, check my blood for sugar, and take insulin shots. That way I stay healthy."
>
> "Can you hang on a sec? I have to eat something before we go shoot baskets. Would you like some crackers too?"
>
> "If my sugar level gets too low, I might start acting confused. That means I'll need to eat something. I usually carry a juice box in my backpack. It would help me a lot if you'd remind me to drink one if I seem sick or act confused."

Your friends will probably ask you lots of questions at first. They may wonder how you got diabetes, or they may want to see you check your blood sugar or take an insulin shot. In fact, shots are probably what most kids will be most curious about. Many kids may wonder if you're going to die, although most probably won't come right out and say this. Head off this worry and ease their concerns by telling them right up front that you plan to live a good long life with diabetes.

Some of their questions may sound stupid, but try not to get annoyed. You probably didn't know much about diabetes either, until you found out you had it! Try to remember that your friends ask questions about your diabetes because they're curious and they care about you. If you're comfortable talking about your diabetes, it can really help get your friendships "back to normal." Sometimes, when everyone *doesn't* talk about a major issue like a friend getting diabetes, it can end up feeling like there's an elephant in the room and no one is discussing it. It becomes a bigger issue than it really needs to be.

On the other hand, don't be surprised if some of your friends don't seem to want to talk much about your diabetes. They could be scared for you, or they may worry that they could catch diabetes from you. They may worry that you'd be uncomfortable talking about it. Try not to let this bother you.

It may be a shock at first for your friends, and it may take them a while to understand. But when they see that you're still the same person you always were, and that you can still do the same things, they'll probably soon forget all about it. Just explain little by little what diabetes is, as it comes up naturally.

CHECKING YOUR BLOOD SUGAR LEVEL AT SCHOOL

Your doctor will probably want you to check your blood sugar during the school day, usually before eating snacks or lunch, before physical activity, or when you've got symptoms of high or low blood sugar. Many students can check their own blood sugar level. Some kids (especially younger students) may need supervision; very young kids will need the nurse or a trained school staffer to check blood sugar for them. It's extremely important that you be allowed to check your blood sugar levels whenever you need to in the classroom or anywhere else in school and during any school activity, and that you be allowed to treat levels that are too high or too low as quickly as possible before symptoms worsen. Because low blood sugar (hypoglycemia) isn't always completely preventable, and not all students will recognize its symptoms with every episode, school personnel should be familiar with the symptoms and treatment so that an urgent problem can be handled in the right way.

SNACKING AT SCHOOL

It's critical that you eat meals and snacks on time; otherwise, you may have a low blood sugar reaction, especially if you missed a morning snack or you were running around a lot during gym. Many parents like to bring a supply of snacks and extra supplies to keep on hand in the classroom and also at the nurse's office.

Some good suggestions for classroom snacks that teachers (or you) can keep on hand include:

- bagels with lowfat cream cheese
- bread sticks
- cereal (dry)
- crackers with peanut butter or cheese filling
- frozen yogurt
- fruit or fruit kabobs
- fruit sorbet
- fruit with plain yogurt
- graham crackers
- muffins
- popcorn
- pretzels
- saltines

While there aren't usually any forbidden foods in a meal plan for kids with diabetes, watch out for parties at school, which often include high-fat, high-carb items.

Once kids at school learn that you need to carry snacks with you for your diabetes, you may find you're constantly being asked for a piece of candy, and this can start to get uncomfortable. While sharing is always a nice thing to do, if you start handing out your snacks you may end up with nothing when you really need it. That's why many kids don't carry candy or snacks with them at school. Instead, some kids put together plastic bags of their favorite candy or items they're most comfortable using (like juice boxes) or complex carbohydrates, such as packets of cheese and crackers, in 15-gram carbohydrate groups. Your teacher, homeroom teacher, or school nurse can keep the bags in a special drawer so you don't have to ask permission; you can just take what you need if your blood sugar is getting low.

But what do you do when you're in high school and you're spending time with five or six different teachers during the day? You might make up special envelopes for every single teacher who'll spend time with you. The envelopes contain a list of symptoms of low blood sugar and include a couple of juice boxes and granola bars.

BEFORE A BIG TEST

It's important that your teachers understand how low blood sugar can affect your ability to think clearly. This can be a real problem if you're about to take a test! You should check your blood sugar level about an hour before a big test, since stress can affect your blood sugar. You also might want to check your blood sugar immediately before the test; if it's low, you should eat a snack and wait 10 minutes before you start the test. Remember, your teachers *must* allow you to do this. Many teachers understand the link between blood sugar and thinking ability and are willing to let you take the test after school or even the next day if you're feeling really foggy.

PLANNING FOR EMERGENCIES

Odds are you're never going to have to use an emergency kit, but still you and your parents need to be prepared in the event of natural disasters or emergencies when you would need to stay at school. Make sure that each year you bring an emergency supply kit from home, which should contain enough supplies for 72 hours. The kit should include the following items (where appropriate):

- blood glucose meter, testing strips, lancets, and batteries for the meter
- urine ketone strips
- insulin and supplies
- insulin pump and supplies, including syringes
- oral medications (if needed)
- antiseptic wipes
- fast-acting sources of sugar—candy, snacks, juice—enough for three episodes
- carbohydrate-containing snacks—enough for three episodes
- glucagon emergency kit

DISCRIMINATION

Sandy's ninth grade history class was all set to go on a tour of their state's capital, an hour's bus ride away from school, but the teacher took him aside and told him he couldn't go unless his mom or dad came too. The teacher was afraid Sandy might have an episode on the trip, and she didn't want the responsibility. Sandy was upset. He didn't want to be treated like a little kid, and he knew none of his friends' parents were going on the trip.

Education Discrimination Materials

The American Diabetes Association can provide information for anyone faced with discrimination at school. You or your parents can call (800) 342-2383 to ask for the association's packet on education discrimination.

Sandy was right to be upset. What he experienced was discrimination, something that happens when people with diabetes aren't treated fairly just because they have diabetes. It usually happens just because people don't know much about diabetes. It's discrimination if you're not allowed to go on field trips or not allowed unless your parent comes too. It's discrimination to be cut from a sport because the coach thinks people with diabetes can't be good athletes. It's discrimination to be told you can't come to school or you can't eat snacks in class or on the bus or to be punished for being absent from school because of diabetes. It's also discrimination to be barred from after-school activities because no one there knows about diabetes care.

Even today, kids with diabetes still face discrimination. For example, some kids may not be given help to monitor their blood sugar or they may not be allowed to eat needed snacks.

LEGAL PROTECTIONS

There are laws that give you the *right* to go to school, play sports, join clubs, go on field trips, and do everything else that kids without diabetes do. Three federal laws address the school's responsibilities to help students with diabetes: Section 504 of the Rehabilitation Act of 1973, the Americans with Disabilities Act (ADA), and the Individuals with Disabilities Education Improvement Act of 2004 (IDEA). These federal laws provide a framework for planning and implementing effective diabetes management at school. As part of these laws, your school also may develop an education plan for you, such as a Section 504 Plan or Individualized Education Program (IEP). These explain what accommodations, education aids, and services you may need because of your diabetes.

Section 504. This law outlines a process that your school can use to determine if you have a student disability and what services you might need. Historically, students with diabetes have been covered by Section 504 and the ADA. Under Section 504, students with disabilities must be given an equal opportunity to participate in academic, nonacademic, and extracurricular activities. You don't have to receive special education services in order to receive related aids and services under Section 504. Administering insulin or glucagon, providing help in checking blood sugar levels, and allowing you to eat snacks in school are a few examples of "related aids and services" that your school must provide if you have diabetes. Most often, these related aids and services are included in a written document called a "Section 504 Plan." Private schools that receive federal funds may not exclude an individual student with a disability if the school can, with minor adjustments, provide an appropriate education for you. Private, nonreligious schools are covered by Title III of the ADA.

IDEA. IDEA provides federal funds to make special education and related services available to eligible children with disabilities. A child with a disability must meet the criteria of one or more of 13 disability categories and need special education and related services. The IDEA category of "other health impairment" includes diabetes as one of the health conditions listed. To qualify under IDEA, however, your diabetes also must adversely affect your educational performance to the point that you need special education and related services. A child with diabetes may qualify under IDEA if he has trouble paying attention or concentrating at school because of recurring high or low blood sugar levels that are hurting school performance.

Your IEP must include the supplementary aids and services to be provided for you, along with a statement of the modifications or supports that will be provided so you can make progress. Administering insulin or glucagon, helping to check blood sugar levels, and letting you eat snacks in school are a few examples of related services, supplementary aids and services, or program modifications or supports that schools can provide if you're eligible under IDEA. However, if you have diabetes but you only need a related service and not special education services, you aren't eligible for any services under IDEA. You still might be eligible for services under Section 504.

Every kid with diabetes has different needs. If your school develops an education-related plan for you, it will probably include details on where and when blood sugar testing and treatment will occur, who is trained to check your blood sugar or give you insulin and glucagon, who is trained to treat hypoglycemia and hyperglycemia, and where your diabetes management supplies will be kept. The plan also will stipulate that you must be given free access to the restroom and water fountain, meals and snacks, and that you must be allowed to participate in all school-sponsored activities and field trips. The plans will provide that you be given makeup tests if you're experiencing hypoglycemia or hyperglycemia and that you be given permission for absences, without penalty, for doctors' appointments and diabetes-related illness.

The information in the Diabetes Medical Management Plan can be used in developing either a Section 504 Plan or an IEP, but should not be a substitute for these plans. If you ever feel that someone is not letting you do something because of your diabetes that you should be allowed to do, the first thing you need to do is talk to your parents. Together you can decide the next step.

If you're facing discrimination. Most people aren't evil at heart. Some may discriminate against people with diabetes and not even realize they're doing it. They may even think they've got your best interests in mind. The solution to this problem is simple: education. Ask your mom or dad or your diabetes educator to discuss your diabetes with the school staffer who's causing the problem. Most of the time, the person stops discriminating once they learn more about diabetes.

Unfortunately, sometimes educating people about diabetes doesn't help, and then you and your parents will need to make some decisions about what to do next. You could have your parents talk to people higher up in the school or the organization, such as the district supervisor or the head of the school board. They might choose to write letters to people who could help, such as an official with a diabetes organization or a state government official. They could contact other parents of kids with diabetes or members of your diabetes support group.

For More Information

For more information or questions about these laws, call (800) 514-0301 or (800) 514-0383 (TDD), or go to the government's Web site at http://www.usdoj.gov/crt/ada/.

If the discrimination continues and you decide it really is intolerable, you and your parents may decide to file an official complaint and use the legal system to make sure that you are treated fairly. Several federal and state laws provide protections to kids with disabilities, including children or teens with diabetes. These laws make sure that children must have full access to public programs, including public schools and most private schools. The laws say that students with diabetes are entitled to accommodations and modifications necessary for them to stay healthy at school and have the same access to an education as other students do.

Your school can prepare a formal plan that outlines how your special health care needs will be met. The plan should identify school staff responsible for making sure the plan is followed, and your parents should be at the meeting when the plan is developed. Any changes to the plan should be made only with your parents' consent. Ideally, the plan should be updated every year.

WHAT YOU NEED TO KNOW

- A diabetes educator who has passed a test about diabetes care is called a Certified Diabetes Educator (CDE).
- A health care plan or a diabetes medical management plan (DMMP) outlines how to manage diabetes at school.
- The DMMP includes your diagnosis date, current health status, emergency contacts, list of diabetes equipment and supplies, and specific medical orders for blood sugar testing and medications to be given at school. It also includes a meal and snack plan, exercise requirements, and a description of and treatment for high and low blood sugar symptoms.
- Your school should have a glucagon emergency kit to be administered by trained school personnel in case your blood sugar ever falls seriously low.
- An emergency kit usually contains a bottle of powdered glucagon and a prefilled syringe with special liquid; the two are mixed just before a glucagon injection is given.
- You and your parents should meet with school staff to discuss your diabetes and how you'll take care of it.
- You and your parents should review your plan each year.

6

You Are What You Eat: Diet Choices for Healthy Blood Sugar

Sharon's favorite meal comes in a paper sack: burger, fries, and a soda grabbed on the run at the drive-up window at her local fast food place. Sharon is a 17-year-old high school junior, so she knows this isn't the healthiest food. But lots of times she skips lunch period at school because she's so busy with extra practices and homework and she's starving by the time school's out. She's about 15 pounds overweight, but she just doesn't think she has the time to eat right.

Sharon doesn't have diabetes yet, but her need to eat a healthy diet is every bit as important as any kid with diabetes. Whether you've got diabetes or not, *all* teenagers need to eat a variety of foods to maintain normal growth and development. The only difference is that the timing, amount, and content of the food that a student with diabetes eats must be carefully balanced.

If you've been diagnosed with diabetes, you probably already know that one of the most important things you can do to stay healthy is to carefully manage your diet, balancing what you eat with insulin injections (if you have Type 1), medications (if you have Type 2), and exercise. How well you can follow your diet and stick to regular mealtimes can really make an important difference in how you feel. A healthy diabetes eating plan isn't weird and doesn't mean you'll have to eat wildly different things from your friends. In fact, if every teenager followed a diabetes diet, they'd all be much healthier!

As soon as you're diagnosed with diabetes, you'll meet with a dietician or diabetes educator to discuss your diet. A certified diabetes educator (CDE) is usually a registered nurse with special training who is certified by the National Board of Diabetes Educators. A dietician, physician, or pharmacist also can be a CDE. Your CDE will help you understand diabetes and teach you how to balance your insulin or pills with food, blood tests, and exercise. A registered dietician (RD) is trained in the field of nutrition (an LD credential means the person is licensed). Many registered dieticians are also CDEs. You'll meet with your dietician once or twice to work out a special meal plan tailored to your situation, taking into account how much you still need to grow, what your lifestyle is like, and what foods you like best, while keeping your blood sugar levels within your target range. Portion size, the right amount of calories for your age, and healthy food choices are also important.

DIABETES AND WEIGHT

If you have Type 1 diabetes, you probably aren't overweight. In fact, weight *loss* is much more likely to be your experience, at least before you're diagnosed, since you don't have enough insulin in your body. However, once you've been diagnosed, if you're getting the right amount of insulin you can gain weight if you eat too much, and this can make it tougher to manage your condition.

If you have Type 2 diabetes, you may well be overweight or even obese, since too much body fat (along with lack of exercise) often triggers this type of diabetes by increasing your body's resistance to the effects of insulin. If you have Type 2 diabetes and you can get your weight under control, you'll also be able to control your blood sugar. In some cases, managing your weight is *all* you have to do in order to normalize your blood sugar. This means you might be able to control your condition with just your diet, so you won't need to take any medicine at all!

More than 15 percent of American teens and children are overweight, and another 15 percent are at risk of becoming overweight, which represents at least 9 million kids, according to government statistics. As a nation, we're eating too much and not exercising enough. This is the main reason experts think so many teenagers are developing Type 2 diabetes.

You probably have already learned the simple chemistry of obesity: If you eat more calories than you burn, you gain weight. But where lots of kids go wrong is in assuming that as long as they're not gulping down entire cartons of Rocky Road or vats of Twinkies, they won't gain weight. The truth is, nutrition experts say that eating just 50 calories extra a day more than you burn will mean you gain a pound a year. That probably doesn't sound like much, but think about it. What if you gain a pound a year every year? If you're 16 and you gain a pound, by the time you're 20 you will have gained five pounds. By age 30, you will have gained 15 pounds. If you do the math, it isn't

Find Your Body Mass Index

Your Body Mass Index (BMI) is a relationship between weight and height that is associated with body fat and health risk. BMI correlates with body fat, although the exact relationship between fatness and BMI differs with age and gender. For example, women are more likely to have a higher percentage of body fat than men.

To figure out your BMI:

1. Multiply your height in inches times your height in inches.
2. Divide your weight in pounds by the product of step 1.
3. Multiply this answer by 703.
4. The answer is your BMI.

For example, if you're 72 inches tall and weigh 180 pounds, here's how you'd get your BMI:

1. 72 inches × 72 inches = 5,184
2. 180 ÷ 5,184 = .0347222
3. .0347222 × 703 = 24.4

Don't like math? Visit the BMI calculator and plug in your height and weight at the Centers for Disease Control (CDC) Web site: http://www.cdc.gov/nccdphp/dnpa/bmi/calc-bmi.htm.

Keep in mind that your BMI will change over the years, and girls and boys have different amounts of body fat as they mature. This is why BMI for teens (also called the BMI-for-age) is different for girls and boys and different for different ages. BMI-for-age is plotted on gender-specific growth charts up to age 20. To check out the 2000 CDC Growth Charts, visit CDC's National Center for Health Statistics at http://www.cdc.gov/growthcharts.

pretty! If you eat 100 extra calories a day, that means you'll gain two pounds a year or 10 pounds from age 16 to 20. This is how just overeating a little can pile on the pounds. Getting enough physical exercise is also important if you have diabetes. The calories you burn as you exercise help prevent you from gaining too much weight, and being physically fit helps insulin work more effectively in your body. We'll discuss that more in the next chapter.

HOW FOOD AFFECTS YOUR BLOOD SUGAR

If you're going to be able to manage your meal plan, it really helps first to understand exactly how food affects your blood sugar level. Food provides sugar for your body, which your body needs to fuel its metabolic processes. In a healthy teenager, insulin helps this sugar get into the body's cells, where the sugar is used for fuel. But if you have diabetes you have a problem with insulin. If you have Type 1 diabetes, you don't have any insulin at all. If you have Type 2, you don't have enough or your body doesn't respond to insulin as it should. The end result is the same for both types: When sugar can't get into your body's cells, it builds up in the bloodstream to dangerously high levels.

The three key factors affecting blood sugar are food, exercise, and insulin. If you have Type 1 diabetes, you'll need to anticipate changes in all three factors so you can control your blood sugar. For example, if you run extra laps after school during basketball practice, you'll either need to take less insulin or eat more carbs than usual, because exercise increases your sensitivity to the effects of insulin and increases your need for energy from food.

Carbohydrates and diabetes. Your body uses carbohydrates (pizza, candy, breads, pasta, and rice) to produce sugar, and you know that untreated diabetics have too much sugar in their blood. This doesn't mean that carbs are bad for you, but they do have the biggest impact on your blood sugar. So you just need to be careful about balancing the carbs you eat with insulin, medication, and exercise.

Carbohydrates are basically starches and sugars. They include grains, cereals, pasta, potatoes, bread, fruit, corn, beans, and various types of sugar: fructose (sugar found in fruit), lactose (sugar in milk), corn syrups, refined sugar, and honey. Furthermore, carbs come in two forms: complex carbohydrates (the carbs that don't taste sweet) and simple sugars (the sweet-tasting items).

Complex carbohydrates take time to be broken down by the body, whereas simple sugars are just that—simple—so they are more quickly broken down by the body. How fast a carbohydrate raises blood sugar levels depends on a variety of factors. First, some foods have more carbohydrates, and the more carbs, the more sugar in your blood. Next, the way that carbohydrates are combined with fat or fiber can slow down their absorption rate. In addition, how much soluble fiber in carbohydrates also affects how quickly they are digested (oats, vegetables, and seeds have lots of soluble fiber). Finally, how you prepare carbohydrates affects how quickly they're digested and how fast sugar is released. Raw foods take longer to digest than cooked food and mashing up the cooked food makes it even more easily digestible. Typically, the more highly processed, refined, or broken down the carb, the more quickly it is digested.

In addition, some carbs are better choices for kids with diabetes than others, because some are more nutritious. For instance, simple sugars usually are found in sweets—candy, pies, and cakes—that don't have as many vitamins, minerals, protein, fiber, and other important nutrients. These empty calorie snacks are full of carbs, but they don't have a lot of nutrition. It's a good idea to limit these. You can have an occasional sugary treat, but it's not something you should focus on. Healthy carbs include whole grains, legumes, fresh vegetables, fresh fruits, and dairy products.

Proteins and diabetes. While carbohydrates are important for people with diabetes because they're the main source of sugar in the body, you also need protein for a healthy, balanced diet. You get protein by eating meat, fish, egg whites, milk, and cheese, as well as beans and legumes. As a teenager, you have an especially high need for protein.

Typical recommendations call for between 10 and 15 percent of your daily diet in protein, but what does that really mean? You can think of it as eating between three to five ounces of lean protein; this would be a small chicken breast, a third of a cup of kidney beans, or a cup of cooked carrots. A little more than half the protein you eat is converted to blood sugar (compared to about 90 percent of carbs). Because protein is digested more slowly than carbohydrates, if you combine the two during a meal, you will slow the absorption of sugar into the blood. If you eat too much protein, it's removed from your body by your kidneys, which—over time—can be hard on these organs. Since people with diabetes can tend toward kidney problems anyway, you'll want to be careful not to eat too much protein and overburden your kidneys.

Fats and diabetes. Too much fat causes obesity, and if you have Type 2 diabetes you need to be particularly careful not to eat more than 20 percent of your calories in fat. (To give you an idea of how unhealthy the typical American diet is, most Americans actually get about half their calories in fat.) Saturated fats are those that are solid at room temperature (such as butter and meat fats, hydrogenated or partially hydrogenated vegetable oils, palm or palm kernel oil, coconut oil, vegetable shortening, and cocoa butter). Polyunsaturated fats are liquid at room temperature (such as oils). Monounsaturated fats get a little harder when refrigerated, but don't turn into solids; they include olive, peanut, and canola oils. Experts generally recommend monounsaturated fats as the healthiest choice because they tend to lower levels of bad cholesterol in the body.

Cholesterol. This fatty substance is produced in your body by the liver, but it's also in some foods that you eat. The saturated fats you eat also tend to raise your cholesterol level. Keep this in mind when reading food labels that may proclaim they are cholesterol free—if they have lots of saturated fat, that will boost your cholesterol level. You need to limit your daily cholesterol count to no more than 300 mg while also limiting your saturated fats.

The cholesterol you produce internally comes in two forms: bad cholesterol (LDL—low-density lipoprotein) and good cholesterol (HDL—high-density lipoprotein). Bad cholesterol will build up on the inside of your blood vessels, leading to hardening of the arteries. Good cholesterol removes debris from the inner arterial walls. A cholesterol test measures your total cholesterol and the ratio of LDL to HDL. The higher your HDL level, the better.

Triglycerides. These fats are found in your blood, produced from the carbohydrates that aren't used to produce blood sugar. High levels of these fats swirling around in your blood is considered to be a harbinger of heart disease and is also linked to insulin resistance. Ideally, you should have no more than 200 mg of triglycerides. Between 200 and 400 is the borderline range and means you need to watch your diet to lower your triglyceride levels. If you lower your fat intake, as well as your carbohydrates and alcohol, you should lower your triglyceride levels.

WHAT'S ON YOUR MEAL PLAN?

The American Diabetes Association recommends that people with diabetes follow an individualized meal plan as an important way to manage diabetes and weight. A meal plan is simply a list of what you can eat and how much you should eat each day. Most meal plans are designed to help you stay within a certain range of carbohydrate, fat, and protein consumption, aiming for high fiber, low simple sugar, low fat (especially saturated fat), and many different kinds of healthy foods.

If you're like most teens, you're probably used to eating lots of soda, chips, cakes, cookies, pizza, burgers, and fries. That's really not a healthy diet for anyone, but if you have diabetes it can cause real problems. The first thing you'll need to do on your new diabetes diet is to replace the sweets and high-fat foods with more fruits and vegetables. (You can still have an *occasional* sweet treat.) What you want to aim for is to include lots of different kinds of healthy foods, without eating too much of any one item. You'll also want to pick foods filled with vitamins, minerals, and fiber, instead of overly processed foods.

You'll probably be directed to eat at least three small or moderate meals daily, along with two or three snacks between meals. This way, you'll avoid a sugar onslaught that you'd get by gobbling large meals filled with sweets. You'll also want to eat about the same amount of food at the same time each day, avoiding eating food with added sugar. When you get thirsty, it's best to drink water and avoid juice, punch, soda, and other high-sugar beverages.

Different diabetes experts have different ideas about meal plans, but typically you will be asked to try to eat between 50 to 60 percent of your calories from carbs, 10 to 15 percent from protein, and 20 to 30 percent from fat. There are a variety of meal plans that accomplish this, including the Exchange System, the Food Guide Pyramid, Rate Your Plate, and Carbohydrate Counting.

Soda Epidemic

One reason for the current teenage obesity epidemic is soda: A 20-ounce can of soda contains about 16.87 teaspoons of sugar. During the past 50 years, soft drink consumption has increased 500 percent, according to the U.S. Department of Agriculture. In 1947, we produced an average of about 100 12-ounce cans for every American; by 1997 it reached almost 575 cans for every man, woman, and child in this country.

EXCHANGE SYSTEM

The old standby meal plan for patients with diabetes is the Exchange System, which focuses on counting the number of servings you can have from each food group (or "exchange list"). Every kid is different, so you'll work with your own diabetes expert to come up with a number of servings per meal from the newly updated meal planning groups: the carbohydrate group, the meat and meat substitute group, and the fat group.

The newly expanded and updated meal planning exchange lists have been published by the American Dietetic Association and the American Diabetes Association (ADA) and are available from your diabetes educator or your dietician. While the basis for meal planning calculations remains the same, according to the ADA, the lists have been grouped to allow more flexibility in choosing foods. Many foods have been added to this revision, reflecting the modern interest in reduced fat and vegetarian food products.

The Carbohydrate Group contains the starch, fruit, milk, other carbohydrates, and vegetable lists. ("Other carbohydrates" is a new addition that provides exchange information for cakes, pies, puddings, and so on. Foods from this list can be substituted for foods from the starch, fruit, or milk lists. Some foods on the "other carbohydrate" lists will also count as one or more fat choices.)

The Meat and Meat Substitute Group contains the very lean, lean, medium-fat, and high-fat meat, and substitute lists.

The Fat Group contains the monounsaturated, polyunsaturated, and saturated fats lists.

Every food in one group can be exchanged for another food in the same group. For example, in the meat group, one ounce of lean beef is the same as one ounce of salmon or a quarter cup of cottage cheese. Therefore, at lunch, you could have *either* a serving of lean meat or a quarter cup of cottage cheese.

FOOD GUIDE PYRAMID

The American Diabetes Association has adapted the traditional Food Guide Pyramid for people with diabetes by making some minor changes and reinforcing healthy eating habits. A new food guidance system replacing the former Food Guide Pyramid was announced in April 2005 by the U.S. Department of Agriculture. The new system, called MyPyramid, provides a set of tools based on caloric requirements to help people make healthy food choices and get regular physical activity. If you're interested in using the interactive MyPyramid, you can check it out at: http://www.mypyramid.gov. The ADA still uses the traditional pyramid, which divides food into six groups. The largest group (grains, beans, and starchy vegetables) is on the bottom, which means you should eat more servings of these foods than of any of the others. The smallest group (fats, sweets, and alcohol) is at the top of the pyramid, which means you should eat very few servings of these foods.

The ADA makes two key changes in the traditional pyramid for diabetes: It adds beans and starchy vegetables such as corn, peas, and potatoes to the grain products of bread, cereal, rice, and pasta, because their carbohydrate and calorie content more closely resembles bread than broccoli. The other key change is to move cheese from the "milk, yogurt, and cheese" area to the "meat, poultry, fish, beans, eggs, and nuts" area, because cheese more closely resembles other protein sources containing fat and relatively few carbs. Your dietician can help you adjust the number of servings and serving sizes from each group to meet your nutritional needs.

COUNTING CARBS

Carbohydrate counting involves calculating the number of grams of carbohydrate or choices of carbohydrate you eat. You can figure this out by reading the nutrition information on food labels.

If you have Type 1 diabetes, you'll use this information to determine the amount of insulin you need to control blood sugar for any given meal or snack. As new insulins are developed and more kids use insulin pumps, doctors and dieticians are recommending basing meal plans on counting carbohydrates. This will give you more flexibility in how much food you eat and when you eat it, because insulin is given to match your food intake. Because carbohydrates are

Artificial Sweeteners

All artificial sweeteners aren't alike. Some (sorbitol, xylitol, and mannitol) actually do contain calories and can affect your blood sugar; they're counted as carbohydrates. Nonnutritive sweeteners (saccharin, aspartame, and sucralose) don't have any calories and don't affect your blood sugar.

the major source of the sugar that appears in the blood after a meal, you'll estimate how much carbohydrate is in your meal and use that estimate to calculate your mealtime insulin dose. For example, for every 15 grams of carbs you eat, you might need to take one unit of insulin.

The glycemic index. The glycemic index of a food assigns a numerical value to that food, which tells you how much it will boost your blood sugar. The glycemic index of all food is compared to the reference food of white bread. If 15 grams of another carbohydrate boosts blood sugar more than 15 grams of white bread, it is considered to have a high glycemic index. If it doesn't increase your blood sugar as much as white bread, it has a lower glycemic index. Low glycemic index foods lower both blood sugar and insulin levels, increase insulin sensitivity, and reduce the amount of calories your body stores as fat.

The idea of figuring out how specific carbs affected blood sugar was established in the early 1980s by David Jenkins, M.D., Ph.D., a nutrition professor at the University of Toronto, who wanted to figure out which foods were best for people with diabetes. Dr. Jenkins discovered that foods such as potatoes, which experts had always figured were a complex carbohydrate, actually boosted blood sugar quickly, whereas other simple carbohydrates appeared to affect blood sugar more slowly. The *American Journal of Clinical Nutrition* lists any food under 55 as a low-glycemic food and anything over 70 as high. But the glycemic index of some foods is surprising. Most of the healthy low-fat, high-fiber foods such as fruits and vegetables have a low glycemic index, and starchy and processed foods such as potatoes and breads have a high glycemic index. But there are surprising exceptions. For example, a couple of raisins has a glycemic index of 64, which is more than a serving of popcorn (55).

There are some drawbacks to the glycemic index. First of all, the glycemic index isn't perfect, because every person's response to food is different. You might be able to eat a potato with little effect on your blood sugar, whereas your friend's sugar level would go through the roof. Some people also find the glycemic index difficult to use.

Glycemic load. In addition to knowing how fast a carbohydrate turns into sugar, you must know how much of that carb is in a serving of food. The glycemic load (GL) offers the answer. For example, you've already learned that the carbohydrate in watermelon has a high glycemic index, but watermelon doesn't have many carbohydrates, so watermelon's glycemic load is relatively low. (A GL of 20 or more is considered high, and a GL of 10 or less is considered to be low.) Foods with a low glycemic load almost always have a low glycemic index, but foods with an intermediate or high glycemic load range from a very low to very high glycemic index.

RATE YOUR PLATE

If the other meal plan methods seem stodgy or boring, you might enjoy using the "rate your plate" method as described by the ADA. To figure out if you're about to eat the right kinds of food, mentally draw a line down through the center of your plate, from top to bottom, dividing the plate in half. Next, draw a line across from left to right, dividing the plate into quarters.

About one-fourth of your plate should be filled with protein (such as meat, fish, poultry, or tofu); another fourth should have grains or starchy foods (rice, pasta, potatoes, corn, or peas). The other half should have non-starchy vegetables such as carrots, cucumbers, lettuce, broccoli, salad, tomatoes, celery, or cauliflower. To this you can add a glass of nonfat milk and a small piece of fruit or a roll.

If your weight is normal and your blood sugar is under control, but you're still hungry after a meal, you can usually eat more food (with adjustment in insulin dosage as needed to handle the extra calories if you have Type 1 diabetes). If you need to lose weight or slow down the rate of weight gain as you grow, then you need to eat less.

EATING HEALTHY FOODS WHEN YOU EAT OUT

Tim was shocked his first night in Paris when his meal consisted of a very small slice of beef, about 12 French fries, and a small salad of fresh greens exquisitely dressed with oil and fresh raspberries. A bottle of water was served as his beverage. There was no gigantic basket of rolls or bread, no 16-ounce steak and large plate of fries, and no appetizer. His surprise was even greater at breakfast. Used to a plate of bacon and eggs, toast, fried potatoes, orange juice, and milk back home, he was startled to find that breakfast consisted of an orange, a piece of French bread, a pat of butter, a small container of preserves, and coffee.

If you've ever traveled in Europe, you may have been surprised to find that what we Americans consider a normal portion at a restaurant is thought of as wildly excessive elsewhere in the world.

Rate Your Plate Interactive Test

For a fun way to test out how well you can "rate your plate," visit ADA's Web site at: http://www.diabetes.org/all-about-diabetes/chan_eng/i3/i3p4.htm.

At Tim's favorite restaurant in the States, he'd start his meal with a salad the size of a dinner plate, loaded with blue cheese dressing, croutons, bacon, eggs, and sliced vegetables. This would be followed by an enormous plate of barbecued ribs, a half-pound of French fries, and about two cups of buttery peas or corn. A huge basket of bread and butter would be left on the table, and dessert would be guaranteed to be something gooey and chocolatey.

It's very easy to overeat when you're dining out, but if you follow your meal plan and you think about what you're doing, it's possible to eat out and still manage to eat well. The key is to know what you're eating and how much. Whenever possible, check out the nutritional facts on the menu or ask your server for details. Some restaurants that don't post this information on the menu do keep a list back in the kitchen.

Beware of jumbo portions. If possible, ask for half a portion; more and more restaurants are offering this. Avoid buffets, because it can be tough to estimate portions and even more difficult to figure out contents of the different foods. While salad bars are often a great choice, don't assume that just because it's sitting out there on the bar with the salad fixings, it's automatically healthy. Some salad bar items (such as potato salad and macaroni salad) are loaded with sugar and mayonnaise. You'll also need to avoid high-fat toppings such as dressings, bacon bits, cheeses, and croutons. Instead, fill up your salad bar plate with carrots, peppers, mushrooms, onions, celery, radishes, broccoli, cauliflower, and spinach.

Stick with foods you recognize and be sure you know what nutrients they contain. Lots of restaurants dedicate a section of their menus to "healthy meals" or "diet plans." You can't go wrong with a steamed vegetable or grilled, skinless chicken breast. Avoid dishes that combine unknown amounts of different foods, because that can make it hard to figure out the nutritional content. Don't be afraid to ask your server how a dish is prepared (that's what they're there for). Skip fried or breaded dishes in favor of baked, grilled, broiled, steamed, or poached. Avoid sauces or gravy and ask for low-fat salad dressings.

What's for dessert? You can still finish your meal with something on the sweet side. Choose sugar-free, fat-free frozen yogurt or fresh fruit. You should skip ice cream in favor of ices, sorbets, or sherbets, which have less fat and fewer calories, but remember that they are full of sugar, so you'll need to work that into your meal plan.

Fast-food choices. One of the hardest things about being a teenager with diabetes is that you don't want to stand out from the crowd, and often the crowd isn't eating healthy foods. There may be times when your friends all want to stop off at a fast-food restaurant, and you don't want to be the one to say "let's not!" Fortunately, it's still possible for you to make reasonably decent choices at a fast-food

Portion Size Equivalents

When it comes to portion size, the National Institutes of Health offers a few guidelines. The following one serving equals:

- one medium piece of fruit, which should be the size of a baseball
- ½ cup of pasta, which is about the size of a half baseball
- one piece of cornbread, which should be the size of a bar of soap
- 1½ oz. of cheese, which should be the size of four stacked dice
- 3 oz. of fish, meat, or poultry, which should be the size of a deck of cards
- 2 tablespoons of peanut butter, which should be the size of a ping-pong ball

restaurant, especially as many are deliberately offering more healthy alternatives on their menu.

If your friends want to stop for breakfast at a fast-food place, you do have options. You can choose some cold cereal with fat-free milk, plain pancakes without butter, or plain scrambled eggs, but limit or avoid bacon and sausage (too much fat!). Go for a plain bagel, toast, or an English muffin, but stay away from the other muffins or Danish, croissants or biscuits (they're loaded with sugar and fat). "Fat-free muffins" may sound like a great idea, but too often they have way too much sugar. Add fruit juice or low-fat or fat-free milk. If it's lunch or dinner, you'll want to avoid the "supersize" options and forgo the cheese and gloppy sauces. Instead, choose grilled or broiled sandwiches with lean roast beef, turkey, unbreaded chicken breast, or lean ham. If it's Mexican fast food, you can order a bean burrito, soft taco, fajita, or other nonfried items. Choose chicken over beef and limit refried beans (or substitute with beans that aren't refried). Lettuce, tomatoes, and salsa are all great choices, but back off on the cheese, sour cream, and guacamole. And while salad is usually a good idea, you'll want to avoid the deep-fried taco salad shells.

You may be surprised to learn that pizza can be a good fast-food choice, if you limit yourself to one or two slices of thin crust pizza with vegetable toppings. Try to avoid ordering meat and extra cheese, all of which add calories, fat, and salt.

When you eat is important. If you require insulin or diabetes medication, you'll also need to think about when you eat as much as what you eat. If a gang of your friends are all eating out, try to make a reservation for your normal mealtime, but bring along a snack in case there's a delay in being seated. Try not to eat at peak busy times, so you won't have to wait for a table when you should be eating. If you realize that your meal is going to be later than usual, eat a fruit or starch serving from that meal—not an extra snack—at your usual mealtime. If it turns out that your dinner may be really late, you can eat your bedtime snack at your usual dinnertime, and your regular dinner at the later hour. However, you may need to adjust your insulin to cope with this change in plans.

HANDLING THE HOLIDAYS

Even if you manage to stick to your meal plan most of the time, the hardest time of the year for most kids is the holidays. Sometimes it seems as if the world is determined to derail your best intentions for healthy eating! What with the special cakes, candy, cookies, sweet treats, and massive amounts of food during Thanksgiving, Christmas, and Hanukkah, it may seem impossible to avoid dietary disaster. You've got invitations to party after party that you just know will be filled with forbidden foods.

First of all, remember that it's important to test your blood sugar a lot during the holidays, when you may be eating more food than normal or eating different food. It's especially important to keep track of your blood sugar during these weeks. The good news is that you don't have to give up your favorite seasonal foods just because you have diabetes. If there's something you want to eat during the holidays, whether it's pumpkin pie, egg nog, or English toffee, you can eat it. You've just got to plan ahead. Your meal plan should be flexible enough to leave room for a bit of variety.

Most people think that sweets are the real no-no for diabetics, but you probably have learned by now that managing diabetes is a lot more complicated than simply sidestepping sugar. You've got to watch *all* your carbohydrates, some of which can trigger a surge in blood sugar every bit as dramatic as a candy cane. What you've got to pay attention to is the *total number* of carbohydrates, not the foods that contain them. Just like the rest of the year, you need to eat a healthy, balanced diet low in saturated fat during the holidays, featuring fiber and complex carbohydrates. The holidays may be a time when you don't have as much control over the food that you're served, but you can still be in charge of what you put in your mouth.

Okay, so you've been invited to a New Year's Eve party, and you know there will be lots of fatty, sugary goodies served. Just be prepared, and figure out in a general way how to balance party carbohydrates, fats, and fiber. Take some time before you leave for the party to guess what kind of food you might be served. For instance, if you know that your best friend always serves your favorite chocolate cake for New Year's Eve, then you can plan your meals and medication during the day so that you can have a slice at the party. Thinking ahead means you won't have to deny yourself when the time comes.

If you're really worried that you won't be able to eat anything at the party, then just have a snack before you leave or bring along something you *know* you can eat. Once you get there, it can be hard to rein yourself in if all of your friends are scarfing down pizza, fried hors d'oeuvres, and delectable desserts. Pay attention to what you're eating, especially if it's the kind of party with bowls of food sitting around or being passed, so that it's easy to graze, taking a bit of food here and there. It may not seem like much, but it can add up. If you're being served at the table, speak up and try to control what's being put on your plate. Say no to seconds and avoid alcohol. When the meal is over, try not to collapse on the sofa in front of the TV. Make a point of trying to get in some exercise; suggest a walk around the block after a big meal.

So far, so good. But life isn't usually quite so simple as you're probably realizing as you learn how to cope with your diabetes. What happens if someone offers you something that isn't part of your meal plan? Most of your close friends and family members probably know better, but what if you're at a large party with people you don't know and someone starts urging you to try something you know isn't a good idea? You could be polite and eat it, but you might pay a price later. If you're comfortable with this, and it doesn't seem too ungraceful, you can simply say "Thanks, it sure looks great, but I have diabetes. I have to watch what I eat." Almost anyone with any sense at all will gracefully accept your comment and not pressure you.

If an entire table is looking at you expectantly when you're offered something forbidden, you may not want to speak up and announce your medical condition for all the world to hear. In this case, you could simply smile and agree to accept a bite. Or you might say you're feeling rather full, but could you have some to take with you? Or, you could accept the food and eat just a bite or two. In these times, almost everyone is dieting, so it's unlikely anyone will harass you about leaving something on your plate.

Many teens find coping with their diabetes to be especially difficult around the holidays. It can be a real pain to have to deal with medication or insulin and to have to constantly monitor what you're eating when everyone around you is running amok through the dessert table. It's easy to get resentful when you see so many other people throwing dietary caution to the winds. As a result, some teens end up eating more than they should or grabbing a few too many sweets. It happens, but the important thing is that you don't get too hard on yourself or give up on your diabetes meal plan altogether. One mistake doesn't mean you've lost the war, and you shouldn't use it as an excuse to totally go wild. Besides, when your nondiabetic friend goes off her diet, the worst she can probably expect is to gain a few extra pounds. The consequences for you are more serious. When you go off your program, and your sugar either plummets or skyrockets, you'll pay an immediate price: You'll feel sick.

WHAT YOU NEED TO KNOW

- One of the most important things people with diabetes can do to stay healthy is to balance what they eat with insulin injections (Type 1), medications (Type 2), and exercise.

- Eating just a little too much more than your body burns off can add extra pounds.
- The three key factors affecting blood sugar are food, exercise, and insulin.
- Your body uses carbohydrates (starches and sugars) to produce sugar, and they have the biggest impact on blood sugar.
- Diabetics need to be careful to balance carbs with insulin, medication, and exercise.
- Carbohydrates include grains, cereals, pasta, potatoes, bread, fruit, corn, beans, and fructose (sugar found in fruit), lactose (sugar in milk), corn syrups, refined sugar, and honey.
- Complex carbohydrates don't taste sweet; simple sugars do.
- Protein (meat, fish, egg whites, milk, cheese, beans, and legumes) are also important for a good diet.
- People with Type 2 diabetes should limit their fat to less than 20 percent of calories.
- Monounsaturated fats (olive, peanut, and canola oils) are the healthiest choice because they tend to lower levels of "bad" cholesterol in the body.
- You should eat at least three small or moderate-size meals daily, along with two or three snacks between meals to avoid a sugar onslaught.
- The standard diabetes diet is based on the Exchange System, which focuses on counting the number of servings you can have from each food group (carbohydrates, meat and meat substitutes, and fats).
- The glycemic index of a food assigns a numerical value to that food, which tells you how much it will boost your blood sugar.
- In addition to knowing how fast a carbohydrate turns into sugar, to really understand its effect on blood sugar you must know how much of that carb is in a serving of food—the glycemic load (GL).
- In the "rate your plate" method of diet control, you mentally dissect your plate into fourths; one-fourth should be filled with protein, another fourth with grains or starchy foods, and the other half with non-starchy vegetables. To this you can add a glass of nonfat milk and a small piece of fruit or a roll.

7

Pump It Up!
Exercise for Diabetics

Sharon was a goalie for her school's field hockey team. Sara specialized in the butterfly stroke. Ian loved to shoot hoops with the guys in his neighborhood. Michaela spent almost every weekend working on dressage with her thoroughbred. Warren plays golf with his dad whenever he can.

All of these teens are active in sports that they love, and each has diabetes. Surprised? You shouldn't be. All kids needs plenty of exercise, but it's even more important if you have diabetes. Physical activity can help your heart and blood vessels stay healthy and help keep your weight normal. Exercise also can directly lower your blood sugar levels, because if you're getting exercise, you're using up more fuel (sugar) to power those activities.

Exercise strengthens muscles, and healthy muscle cells more readily absorb insulin, according to research. The fat in your body acts only as a kind of fuel warehouse, storing calories as fat for future use. It's your muscles that are metabolically active, burning calories for energy; the stronger and healthier your muscles, the better they'll be at burning calories. That's why your doctor will tell you to keep on participating in gym classes and team sports even after you've been diagnosed with diabetes, and why your school can't legally stop you from playing sports or participating in gym class.

As we've discussed, your body needs insulin to help transport sugar from the blood to your body's cells where it's used for energy. Without insulin, the sugar in the blood can become dangerously high, the cells of the body don't get enough fuel, and you can experience a life-threatening coma. If you're too heavy, the excess weight can decrease the body's response to insulin; this is known as insulin resistance, which is associated with several health problems.

SWING HIGH, SWING LOW: EXERCISE AND BLOOD SUGAR

When you begin to exercise, your muscles need more fuel to meet the increased demands of your body. To power the body, your muscles tap into your supply of glycogen stored in fat and absorb more circulating sugar in your blood. The harder or longer you exercise, the more energy your body needs, and the more sugar will be absorbed. As you exercise, your blood also circulates faster throughout your body, so any injected insulin will be absorbed more quickly (especially if it was injected into a part of the body that's actively engaged during exercise). As you continue to exercise and your insulin is absorbed, the levels of insulin rise and the liver stops releasing stored sugar, which leads to a subsequent drop in blood sugar.

Hypoglycemia (very low blood sugar) can develop during exercise, when your insulin is being absorbed quickly and when the sugar in your blood is being used more quickly to power the body. Low blood sugar can occur even more quickly if you haven't eaten much before you started exercising.

While low blood sugar is much more common during exercise than high blood sugar, hyperglycemia *can* occur in some cases. If you have diabetes and your insulin levels are low before you start exercising,

The Exercise/Insulin/Blood Sugar Balance

While you exercise, you must balance the following factors:

- blood sugar levels before exercise
- time of last insulin injection
- time since last meal or snack
- intensity and length of exercise

the liver will release a burst of stored sugar, which can lead to a spike in blood sugar as you exercise. This high level of sugar in the blood can last for several hours after you've stopped the activity.

GETTING STARTED

Balancing your blood sugar and insulin needs during exercise can seem a bit scary at first, but it certainly can be done as long as you follow a basic plan. If you've recently been diagnosed with diabetes, your educator or diabetes specialist should suggest an exercise program for you. In fact, some exercise specialists can design unique exercise programs just for kids with diabetes. Before you put on your workout clothes, remember that any exercise plan must first have the approval of your doctor.

Get your doctor's okay. Your doctor must approve any exercise plan, based on the type of exercise you want to do and the condition of your heart, blood vessels, eyes, kidneys, feet, and nervous system. You may need to have an exercise stress test to see how your heart reacts to exercise. If the tests show signs of disease, find out what exercises or activities you can do safely, without making your conditions worse. Your doctor may want to thoroughly check out your blood pressure and heart rate before you start exercising, since high blood pressure can worsen many of the problems linked to diabetes. Your systolic blood pressure (that's the top number in a blood pressure reading) shouldn't top 180 when you exercise.

Find an exercise expert. If you don't have much experience with formal exercise, you could visit a health club, exercise class, or community recreational center for some guidance and direction. You'll want to be sure that the exercises you do are correct and safe. Ideally, your exercise coach or teacher should be certified by a group such as the American College of Sports Medicine or the American Council on Exercise. Some exercise coaches have degrees in sports medicine, exercise physiology, or physical therapy.

Well-trained instructors emphasize improving and maintaining your health and create different exercises depending on the intensity you're looking for. A fitness instructor can design workouts to help you get the most out of your exercise, whether you're at a beginner, intermediate, or advanced level. The class shouldn't exhaust you, and you shouldn't feel pain during or after class.

Best exercises. The best type of exercise is aerobic—that is, any type of exercise in which you work your large muscles using rhythmic movements, so that your heart rate rises, you start to sweat lightly, and your breathing speeds up a bit. Moderation is the key here! Lots of exercises are aerobic: biking, hiking, jogging, dancing, brisk walking, cross-country skiing, or taking an aerobics class. Whatever you do, it should be challenging but not exceedingly difficult.

Ideally, you should get some sort of exercise at least three times a week (although five times is better!) for between 20 minutes to an hour. Be careful not to fall into that "all or nothing" pattern. Five times a week is great, and three times a week is good, but *some* exercise is always better than *no* exercise. If you only have time for a walk around the block once a week, then that's where you should start. Grab your iPod and start warming up those muscles. Once you get into the routine, you may be able to increase the intensity, the length of time, or the number of days in which you exercise. In addition to formal exercise, try to pack in other exercise throughout the day by walking instead of driving; taking the stairs instead of the elevator; working on the lawn or cleaning your room every day. If you drive to school, park at the far end of the lot and walk to the building. Remember, you can burn calories just as easily by doing these types of non-exercise exercise.

Keep these exercise tips in mind.

- Eat a meal between one and three hours before you start your aerobic exercise.
- If you take insulin, inject a dose at least one hour before you begin. If you've forgotten and you need to inject more quickly than that, then you should inject in a part of the body that won't be moving (avoid the thigh, for example).
- Remember to decrease the insulin dose before exercise, per your doctor's instructions.
- Check your blood sugar level. If it's higher than 250 mg/dl, delay your exercise.
- Warm up your muscles for about five or 10 minutes. This will allow your heart and breathing to gradually slow down and will help prevent stiffness and muscle pain.
- Eat a carb supplement at least every half hour during exercise if you're exercising vigorously (say, you're playing a rough game of basketball) or you're exercising for a long time.
- Check your blood sugar level during exercise.
- Cool down for about five or 10 minutes at the end of your exercise period.

Check Your Blood Sugar Often!

Everyone's blood sugar level responds differently to exercise. To learn how your body responds, check your blood sugar before and after exercise. The more you know about your body's response to exercise, the better you will be able to control your blood sugar level. Also check your blood sugar during exercise any time that you notice symptoms such as hunger, nervousness, shakiness, or sweating. If your blood sugar is 70 or below:

- Swallow two to five glucose tablets.
- Drink ½ cup (4 ounces) of fruit juice or a regular soft drink.
- After 15 minutes, check your blood sugar again. If it's still below 70, have another serving and repeat these steps until your blood sugar is at least 70.

- Check your blood sugar level.
- Eat more for up to 24 hours after exercise, depending on how intense your workout was and how long you exercised.
- Your gym teachers and your coaches should be trained to recognize low blood sugar and help treat you if necessary. You must always keep a quick-acting source of sugar and your blood sugar meter available, along with plenty of water, as you exercise.

LET'S GET SPECIFIC: EXERCISE FOR TYPE 1 DIABETES

Exercise is important for everyone with diabetes, but if you have Type 1 diabetes, you'll need to make sure that you keep your blood sugar levels within a safe range while you're working out. If your fasting blood sugar level is above 250 and you have ketones in your urine, you should avoid exercise.

Since exercise lowers blood sugar levels, you'll need to adjust what you eat and how much insulin you take. To prevent your blood sugar from getting too low, you may need to check it more often while you're exercising. Exercise is still important if you have Type 1 diabetes, as long as you can figure out how to balance your food and insulin requirements. Exercise can affect your blood sugar levels for between six to eight hours afterward, but if you're a regular exerciser, your levels may stay low for up to 36 hours!

What you really want to avoid is having your blood sugar get too low during exercise. Let's say you're going to participate in an energetic gym class featuring weight training for 30 minutes. First, test your blood sugar level; if the sugar is low, eat a snack right before gym. Eating a snack right beforehand is also a good idea if you want to keep your blood sugar level stable as you're exercising. As you begin the class, make sure you keep a snack nearby in case your blood sugar levels fall, and make sure that your teacher knows how to spot when you're having a hypoglycemic episode. After class, test your blood sugar again. If you're going to exercise for more than an hour (say, you're going for a long bike ride or an energetic trail ride on horseback), check your blood sugar during the exercise.

Your doctor will recommend whether you should adjust your insulin doses before or after exercise (or both). It's important to discuss exercise and your insulin requirements with your doctor; he or she will explain how to change your insulin treatment when you exercise. You should never try to make those changes on your own. If you use an insulin pump, you may disconnect the pump for sports activities, but if you keep the pump on, you can set the pump to deliver a temporary lower rate of insulin while you're playing. Again, your doctor will work with you on this.

Get the Right Shoes!

Foot problems can be a major hassle in people with diabetes. If you're going to be exercising, be sure to wear top-quality, properly fitting exercise shoes designed for the correct activity. Shoes should be canvas or leather (your feet need to breathe), and you should always wear seamless sports socks. You might want to have your diabetes specialist or a podiatrist check your shoes for a proper fit.

LET'S GET SPECIFIC: EXERCISE FOR TYPE 2 DIABETES

Because people with Type 2 diabetes can directly influence the course of their disease by getting exercise and losing weight, getting out there and exercising is especially important if you have this type of diabetes.

Exercise improves the ability of your muscles to absorb sugar and reduces insulin resistance. Here's why: As you exercise, your muscles need more energy, so they absorb more sugar from your blood. The more you exercise, the more your muscle cells will get used to responding to insulin. Some experts suspect that regular exercise actually stimulates your muscle cells to develop more insulin receptors, so that more sugar can be absorbed! If you have Type 2 diabetes, this insulin response is typically sluggish. So you'll want to do anything you can to rev up your body's sensitivity to insulin. In addition, as you exercise and eat more healthy foods, you'll probably lose weight, including fat, and the less fat you have, the less insulin you'll need.

If you have Type 2 diabetes, you probably aren't taking insulin, so your blood sugar probably won't react quite so much to exercise. This doesn't mean you can ignore hypo- or hyperglycemia, however! Some kids who take diabetes medication still need to adjust their dosage on days when they get a lot of exercise. Your doctor is the best person to advise you on this.

If you have Type 2 diabetes, here are some tips to keep in mind while exercising:

- Wait between one to three hours after eating before exercising.
- Check your blood sugar level about 30 minutes before exercising; if it's less than 100 mg/dl, you should eat a snack and then wait about 15 to 30 minutes before exercising; check your blood sugar again before starting to exercise.
- If your level is above 200 mg/dl, check your urine for ketones. If the test is negative, go ahead and start exercising.

LIFTING OR JOGGING: WHICH EXERCISES ARE BEST?

There isn't a diabetes-specific exercise that's better for you than another. Any moderate aerobic exercise is a good choice, and the intensity of the workout depends on your goals and your overall physical condition. Whatever you do, it's important to choose something you enjoy; forcing yourself to run every day when you loathe running will make it harder for you to keep up with your exercise regimen. If you prefer swimming, biking, or aerobics class, then select those activities instead.

Some kids find stopping to take their heart rate is a hassle and can learn how to judge the intensity of their exercise by other methods. Your body will tell you how hard it's working during exercise if you learn how to listen. If you're still able to hold a conversation (although you need to take an extra breath every few words), you're getting a moderately intense aerobic workout. If you're exercising so

Figuring Out Your Heart Rate

You'll need to check your heart rate to make sure you're exercising enough but not too much. To figure out what your maximum heart rate should be:

- Subtract your age from 220.
- Multiply this number by .65 and by .8.
- This gives you the low and high heart rate range you aim for during moderate exercise.

For example, if you're 16, here's how to find your maximum heart rate:

1. 220 − 16 = 204
2. 204 × .65 = 133
3. 204 × .8 = 163

For a low-intensity workout, your heart rate should be about 133 beats per minute; for a high-intensity workout, the heart rate should be about 163. To find what your heart rate should be for a brief 10-second check, divide each by 6: 133 ÷ 6 = 22.1; 163 ÷ 6 = 27.1.

So for a moderate-intensity workout at age 16, your heart rate after checking your pulse for 10 seconds should be between 22 and 27 beats.

hard that all you can do is pant and there's no way you could talk, you're exercising so hard you're not doing aerobic exercise. On the other hand, if you can chat or sing so easily you don't need an extra breath at all, you're not exercising hard enough to get any aerobic benefit.

Strength training. Strength training helps build strong bones and muscles, and with more muscles, you'll burn more calories. You can learn how to do strength training at school (many gym programs offer "weight training" or "strength training" classes). Or you can join an exercise class at an exercise club, the local gym, or the YMCA/YWCA, working with weights. Once you learn the right technique, you can practice lifting weights at home.

WHO SHOULDN'T EXERCISE

In general, any teenager with diabetes should be exercising, except for those with certain conditions such as uncontrolled blood sugar, heart disease, certain eye disorders, or numbness in their feet or legs.

Fluctuating blood sugar. If your blood sugar is all over the map, spiking up and plummeting down all day long, your doctor probably won't want you to do intensive physical exercise until you can achieve a bit better control of your condition.

Eye problems. Exercise can complicate an eye condition called proliferative retinopathy (a condition of fragile blood vessels, with potential high pressure and hemorrhaging into the eye). Any kind of exercise involving heavy lifting or straining or pressure on the abdomen could briefly increase pressure in the eye, heightening the risk of hemorrhage.

Heart disease. Kids with diabetes might want to get a stress test before starting an exercise program to make sure the heart hasn't already suffered some mild, unforeseen damage. Your doctor can help you devise an exercise program that won't be too intense for your heart.

Numbness. If your legs or feet are numb, it's much more likely that you'll sustain an injury or joint damage. Make sure to wear top-quality exercise shoes or sneakers and be careful about not doing too much jogging or running.

EXERCISE AS PREVENTION

For those who are at risk for Type 2 diabetes, just 30 minutes of exercise a day (or even just one hour a week, according to new research) can make a big difference in preventing the disease. Studies have shown that if you're an overweight teen, losing excess poundage by getting exercise can improve insulin sensitivity. The more weight you lose (until you get to a normal level) the better, because if you're really overweight but you only drop a couple of pounds, your insulin sensitivity won't improve that much.

WHAT YOU NEED TO KNOW

- Physical activity can help your heart and blood vessels stay healthy and help keep your weight normal and directly lowers your blood sugar levels.
- If you have diabetes, your school can't legally stop you from playing sports or participating in gym class.
- Exercise strengthens muscles, and healthy muscle cells more readily absorb insulin.
- During exercise, muscles need more fuel to meet the increased demands, so muscles tap into the supply of glycogen stored in fat, as well as absorbing more circulating sugar in blood.
- The harder or longer you exercise, the more energy your body needs, and the more sugar will be absorbed.
- During exercise, blood circulates faster so any injected insulin will be absorbed more quickly (especially if it was injected into a part of the body that's actively engaged during exercise).
- As exercise continues and insulin is absorbed, the levels of insulin rise and the liver stops releasing stored sugar, which leads to a subsequent drop in blood sugar.
- Hypoglycemia can develop during exercise when insulin is absorbed quickly and the sugar in blood is being used more quickly to power the body.
- Low blood sugar can occur even more quickly if you haven't eaten much before you started exercising.
- Low blood sugar is much more common during exercise than high blood sugar, but hyperglycemia *can* occur in some cases.
- You must balance blood sugar levels before exercise, time of last insulin injection, time since last meal or snack, and intensity and length of exercise.
- The best type of exercise is aerobic, in which large muscles use rhythmic movements so heart rate rises, you start to sweat lightly, and your breathing speeds up a bit.

- Ideally, you should get some sort of exercise at least three times a week (although five times is better!) for between 20 minutes to an hour.
- You shouldn't exercise if you have uncontrolled blood sugar, heart disease, certain eye disorders, or numbness in the feet or legs.
- People can prevent Type 2 diabetes by just 30 minutes of exercise a day (or even just one hour a week, according to new research).

8

Medication: Oral Drugs and Insulin

You can make a big difference in your chance of staying healthy by keeping your blood sugar levels as close to normal as possible. If you have diabetes, you can do that by eating right, getting lots of exercise, losing extra weight, and keeping your blood pressure, cholesterol, and triglyceride levels low.

If you have Type 1 diabetes, you'll need an insulin pump or insulin injections, and if you have Type 2 diabetes, you may need to use either medication or (much less often) insulin. Today, kids with diabetes have more options for blood sugar testing and insulin administration than ever before. With proper daily care and treatment, you can still lead a healthy, active, fun-filled life.

TREATMENT FOR TYPE 2 DIABETES

Many teens with mild to moderate Type 2 diabetes (defined as a fasting glucose level of 126 to 140) can control their disease with exercise and simple changes in diet. Pills are especially effective if your blood sugar isn't too high or if you've just been diagnosed. But if that's not enough to control your blood sugar or if your diabetes is more severe (fasting glucose level of 141 to 180), there are a variety of effective medications available. Since the mid-1990s, many medications have been introduced to treat Type 2 diabetes at the level of insulin resistance. These are NOT pill forms of insulin. They are a separate group of medications that include five classes of drugs:

- thiazolidinediones
- biguanides
- sulfonylureas
- meglitinides
- alpha-glucosidase inhibitors

Thiazolidinediones and biguanides. These insulin sensitizers are typically the drug doctors prescribe first to address the basic problem with this condition. This medication makes your body more sensitive to insulin. The thiazolidinediones are a group of insulin sensitizers including rosiglitazone (Avandia), troglitazone (Rezulin), and pioglitazone (ACTOS), which help insulin work better in the muscle and fat and also reduce sugar production in the liver. You should take these drugs once or twice a day with food. Although they are good at lowering blood sugar, they can have a rare but serious effect on the liver. For this reason, your doctor will perform blood tests regularly to monitor the health of your liver.

Metformin (Glucophage) is a type of drug called a biguanide, which lowers blood sugar mostly by decreasing the amount of sugar produced by the liver. Metformin also helps to lower blood sugar by making muscle tissue more sensitive to insulin so sugar can be absorbed. It's usually taken two times a day. Metformin may cause diarrhea, but this side effect can improve if you take the drug with food.

Sulfonylureas and meglitinides. These two groups of drugs work in a different way, allowing your pancreas to produce more insulin by stimulating the insulin-producing cells in the pancreas (the beta cells). As the cells produce more insulin, the level of sugar in your blood should drop.

Sulfonylurea drugs have been prescribed since the 1950s. Chlorpropamide (Diabinese) is the only first-generation sulfonylurea still used today. The three second-generation sulfonylureas, which are used in smaller doses, include glipizide (Glucotrol and Glucotrol XL), glyburide (Micronase, Glynase, and Diabeta), and glimepiride (Amaryl). These drugs are typically taken once or twice daily before meals. All sulfonylurea drugs have about the same effect on blood sugar, but they have different side effects and interactions and are taken in different amounts.

Meglitinides also stimulate the beta cells to release insulin. Repaglinide (Prandin) and nateglinide (Starlix) are meglitinides that are taken before each of three meals.

Because sulfonylureas and meglitinides stimulate the release of insulin, it's possible to experience low blood sugar as a result. When you're taking these drugs, you shouldn't drink alcohol. Sometimes chlorpropamide or other sulfonylureas can cause vomiting, flushing, or sickness.

Alpha-glucosidase inhibitors. This class of drugs, which delay the absorption of carbohydrates in the small intestine, includes acarbose (Precose) and meglitol (Glyset). These drugs help lower blood sugar by blocking the breakdown of carbohydrates such as bread, potatoes, and pasta in the intestine and slowing the breakdown of some sugars, such as table sugar. This carb blocking slows the rise in blood sugar after a meal. These medications should be taken at the very beginning of a meal. These drugs may have side effects, including gas and diarrhea.

MIX 'N' MATCH

The different classes of diabetes drugs act in different ways, so you can combine two or more to get better blood sugar control. For example, many patients mix a biguanide and a sulfonylurea together. Some people find that after taking oral medications for years, they suddenly stop working. When this happens, doubling up on two different medications may be more effective. Although taking more than one drug can be more expensive and can increase the risk of side effects, switching from a single medication to another isn't typically as effective as combining two types of diabetes medicine.

RECENTLY APPROVED INJECTABLE

The U.S. Food and Drug Administration has recently approved exenatide (Byetta), a new class of drugs called incretin mimetics for the treatment of Type 2 diabetes. It's usually prescribed for patients who haven't responded to metformin, a sulfonylurea, or a combination of metformin and a sulfonylurea. Exenatide is a synthetic version of a naturally occurring hormone that was first isolated from the saliva of the Gila monster. This drug is not insulin. Instead, it lowers blood sugar primarily by boosting insulin secretion. Because it only does this when there are high blood sugar levels, it doesn't usually increase the risk of low blood sugar. It may cause nausea, which tends to improve over time. You should inject exenatide with meals. Patients using this drug usually lose some weight in addition to being better able to control blood sugar levels.

OTHER DRUGS

To help protect against heart and circulatory problems, your doctor may recommend that you take a low daily dose of aspirin (unless you're allergic to it). Your doctor may recommend a group of blood pressure drugs called ACE inhibitors that have been shown to protect the heart and the kidneys of people with diabetes. Some doctors also recommend a group of drugs called statins, which are used to lower cholesterol and—in people with diabetes—to alter the inflammatory reaction in the blood vessels.

THE NEXT STEP: INSULIN

If these medications, in combination with diet and exercise changes, don't help you lower your blood sugar, the next step is insulin. Even if diabetes pills work for you, you may need insulin if you have a severe infection or you need surgery. During these physically challenging periods, pills may not be able to control your blood sugar. With many varieties of insulin on the market today, ranging from fast-acting to long-acting, insulin often helps achieve good control of blood sugar levels. At the moment, insulin is only available by injection, although researchers are working hard to develop other, simpler ways of administering the drug. (You can read more about insulin in the next section.) And of course, kids with Type I diabetes will need to use insulin as well.

Insulin Allergy

Sometimes, a person can develop a sensitivity to insulin because it's made from pork or beef or it's not the same as human insulin. The allergy can cause red, itchy skin around the injection site, which is called a local allergy. More seriously, the allergy may be bodywide (systemic), triggering hives or red patches all over the body, along with altered heartbeat and breathing. A doctor may treat this allergy by prescribing purified insulins or by desensitization.

TYPE 1 DIABETES: USING INSULIN

If you have Type 1 diabetes, you'll need to take insulin shots or use an insulin pump, in addition to eating a healthy diet, cutting down on sweets and sugary foods, getting lots of exercise, and controlling your blood pressure.

People with Type 1 diabetes need to inject insulin because their body no longer produces it on its own. Basically, by injecting insulin, you're mimicking the action of your pancreas, which in a healthy person releases a constant amount of insulin, bolstered by extra insulin whenever blood sugar levels start to rise. When you inject insulin (or use an insulin pump), you're providing that constant amount of insulin, and you're also providing the burst of insulin when your blood sugar rises (most typically, after you eat).

Your diabetes medical management plan will outline the correct dosage, delivery system, and schedule for insulin administration, which is tailored to your specific needs. Today, it's easier than ever before to keep your blood sugar level within range with the new types of insulin and new delivery systems.

Several different kinds of insulin are used together to treat people with diabetes. These different types of insulin have been manufactured either to be immediate (rapid-acting and short-acting insulin), intermediate, or long-acting insulin. A coordinated combination of insulins is used to allow for adequate treatment of diabetes at meals, snacks, during periods of physical activity, and through the night. Most insulin today is synthetic human insulin, which is typically more quickly absorbed than animal insulin.

TYPES OF INSULIN

Before you administer insulin, you need to know its onset, the peak time, and the duration. "Onset" refers to how long it takes after an injection for the insulin to reach your blood and start lowering your blood sugar level. "Peak time" is the moment when insulin is at its strongest and most able to lower blood sugar. Its "duration" is the time that insulin continues to lower blood sugar levels.

Rapid-acting insulin (Novolog and Humalog). These two insulins last for between three and five hours. Novolog acts more quickly (its onset is within 10 to 20 minutes), with a peak between one and three hours. Humalog's onset is between 15 and 30 minutes, with a peak at 30 minutes to two-and-a-half hours.

Short-acting insulin. Regular insulin (Humulin R, Novolin R, Velosulin human) is effective within 30 minutes to an hour, peaks in two to four hours, and lasts for six to eight hours.

Intermediate-acting insulin. This includes NPH (Humulin N, Novolin N) and lente (Humulin L, Novolin L), both of which last for between 18 and 24 hours. Onset for both is about one to two hours. Lente peaks between three and 10 hours. NPH peaks between four and 12 hours. Lente, however, is being phased out and is no longer being manufactured.

Long-acting insulin. This includes lantus (Levemir) and ultralente (Humulin U). Onset for ultralente is between 30 minutes and three hours and for lantus is two hours. Lantus lasts for between 18 to 24 hours and ultralente lasts for 20 to 36 hours. There is no peak time for lantus; peak time for ultralente is between 10 and 20 hours. Ultralente, however, is being phased out and is no longer being manufactured.

MIXING INSULINS

At the prebreakfast injection, many people mix a short- or rapid-acting insulin with an intermediate-acting insulin to get a quick spurt of insulin to cover breakfast with an extended benefit that can provide coverage through lunch. You can buy premixed preparations or you (or your parents) can mix insulins yourself. You wouldn't typically mix long-acting insulin with regular (or short-acting) insulin, since this can interfere with its absorption. (If you did want to take them at the same time, you would use a separate injection.) Of course, you should never mix any insulin without the approval of your doctor, who will show you exactly how to mix the two. (The clear faster-acting insulin must always be placed in the syringe first, followed by the longer-acting cloudy insulin.)

ADMINISTERING INSULIN

Because every person with diabetes has a slightly different reaction to insulin, it's important for you to know (by checking your blood sugar) how insulin affects *you*. The three most common ways to administer insulin are with a syringe, an insulin pen, or an insulin pump.

INJECTING INSULIN

As your doctor or diabetes educator should explain, you'll inject your insulin into the fat (not the muscle) just under the skin. The abdomen is the most common area (avoiding the navel), because that's the spot where the insulin is most quickly and evenly absorbed. This is followed in speed of absorption by the upper underarms, the upper or outer thighs, and the buttocks. Most doctors recommend using one part of the body consistently, to keep the level of insulin more even, but rotating sites within that area. Injecting into a body part that is moving during exercise (such as the thigh) will speed up absorption. Absorption will also be faster if you inject while the body is hot (such as after a shower), because the veins will have dilated. Pay attention where you inject depending on how fast you need the insulin to be absorbed.

Insulin syringes

Insulin syringes available today make it easier to draw up the proper dosage, and shorter, smaller needles make injections easier and relatively painless. Most insulin sold in the United States comes in 100 unites per milliliter of fluid (U-100). Automatic injectors can insert the needle painlessly, and some will even insert the insulin for you. Jet injectors are expensive, but some teens like them because they eliminate the needle altogether. Instead, a jet injector sends a high-pressure "shot" of insulin through the skin. The downside to these products is that they can cause bruising, and they must be taken apart for frequent cleaning.

Insulin pumps

More and more teens are choosing insulin pumps as a means to keep blood sugar levels in better control. An insulin pump is a computerized device that looks like a pager and is usually worn on your waistband, pocket, or belt. The pump is programmed to deliver small,

Injection Warning

If you inject insulin at the same spot all the time, you might develop lumps (called lipohypertrophy) or depressions (lipoatrophy) below the surface of the skin. Both lumps and depressions are harmless. You can lessen the risk of this problem by rotating the injection sites. Using purified insulins also may help.

steady doses of fast-acting insulin throughout the day; you add additional doses to cover food or high blood sugar levels. You can also program the pump to deliver different amounts of insulin as needed. The pump holds a reservoir of insulin that is attached to a tube system called an infusion set.

Most infusion sets start with a guide needle, which you insert in the skin (you'll rotate your infusion site between your abdomen, buttocks, and thigh). The plastic cannula (a tiny flexible plastic tube) is left in place, taped with dressing, and the needle is removed. The injection site is usually changed every couple of days or when blood sugar levels remain above target range. Be sure to keep the site clean with soap, water, and alcohol wipes, and always wash your hands when changing infusion sets. If your infusion site is painful or red, remove the infusion set immediately, apply wet, warm cloths, and check with your doctor to make sure you don't have an infection.

Right before meals, you should check your blood sugar level and then give yourself an additional burst of insulin. You also should check your blood sugar level about three or four hours after a meal.

Many kids with diabetes find that living with a pump isn't very difficult. You can easily detach the pump for swimming or showering. At night, you can put the pump on your bedside table, beside you on the bed, under your pillow, or in a pajama pocket. A specific sleeping rate can help keep your blood sugar under control all night, so you'll feel better in the morning and prevent your blood sugar from rising early in the morning.

Hyperglycemia and the pump. If your blood sugar gets too high even with the pump, make sure your pump and infusion set are working properly. Together with your doctor, you can work out how much of an additional dose to take to lower your blood sugar. An hour after giving yourself the extra insulin, you can recheck your blood sugar. If it's still high, your infusion set may not be working. In that situation, you should give yourself a shot of fast-acting insulin and check for ketones in your urine. After changing your infusion set and checking your blood sugar in an hour, you should call your doctor if you start feeling sick.

Hypoglycemia and the pump. The best way to prevent low blood sugar is to check your blood sugar often. If your blood sugar gets too low, you can slow down or stop your insulin by adjusting the pump, and eat some emergency sugar or drink some juice. However, be careful not to *overtreat* low blood sugar. Working with your doctor, you can figure out how much sugar you need to bring your level back to normal. If necessary, you may need to suspend the pump use until your blood sugar gets closer to normal. (You won't need to reprogram the pump when you start again.)

Pump v. injections. About 250,000 people around the world use an insulin pump, and studies show that the pump results in better blood sugar control for teens with diabetes. Insulin pumps are designed to deliver only fast-acting insulin, which is much more predictable. With a pump, you can plan your meals and activities knowing far more accurately when your insulin will take effect. Unlike injections, you can stop or slow the delivery rate if your blood sugar is low, or if you think it might get low.

Insulin absorption from an injection is more unpredictable, which is one of the major reasons that people who inject insulin note their blood sugar can vary so much from day to day. Injections introduce a fairly large amount of insulin all at once, which may be absorbed more slowly if you're not active and more rapidly if you are. An insulin pump delivers a much smaller amount of insulin on a constant basis 24 hours a day, much as a normal pancreas would do. With the press of a button, you can deliver additional insulin to cover meals.

Playing sports. If you play sports, you can detach the pump for a period of time. If you're going to be off the pump for less than an hour, you won't need to make any insulin adjustments. Some kids take a small additional burst of insulin with a snack right before detaching their pump, if they know it will be off for a longer period.

If you wear your pump during sports, you may need to reduce the insulin rate. You'll need to test your blood sugar a few times to figure out what works best for you.

Wearing the pump at school. When you first get a pump, your parents should contact your school and make sure the nurse understands how to use it. You and your parents also will need to update your diabetes management plan to include information about the pump. You should make sure to have extra pump supplies at school, including an extra supply of insulin and an extra infusion set, alcohol wipes, extra batteries, and an insulin syringe or pen injector in case something happens to the infusion set.

Pros and cons. The pumps aren't for every teenager. They are expensive (about $5,000), although many insurance plans cover them. Maintenance can add another $300 a month. It also takes some time to learn how to use the pump, change the programs, and add surges of insulin before meals. You'll also need frequent extra visits to make sure the pump delivers the correct amounts of insulin. Using the pump also means you need to be good at counting carbs at your meals so you can give yourself the correct extra dose of insulin. Physically, there's a risk of infection, and you'll be at risk of high blood sugar if any problem with the device, such as clogged tubes, develops.

All of that sounds scary, but there are also plenty of good reasons to use the pump, especially if you need to carefully control your blood sugar. First, you won't have to give yourself injections, and the near-normal control of blood sugar means fewer complications when you get older. Many teenagers find they need less insulin because the pump administers smaller amounts of insulin. Because insulin use is timed to meals, your schedule can be much more flexible.

Insulin pens

An insulin pen looks sort of like a fountain pen. It holds a cartridge of insulin and uses disposable needles that get screwed onto its tip just before use. Some pens use replaceable insulin cartridges, and others have a non-replaceable cartridge that can be thrown away after use. Insulin pens are convenient and most appropriate when you need a single type of insulin. Pens are the most common insulin delivery system in most of the world, except the United States, where syringes and insulin vials remain more popular.

Prefilled pens using premixed insulin are usually marketed for use by people with Type 2 diabetes. The fixed ratio of insulins does not provide the flexibility needed to accommodate varying food and exercise.

Once the cartridge is loaded into the pen, you screw on a needle, prime the cartridge to clear out air, dial in the desired dose, inject the needle, and press the button to deliver the insulin. If you use a pen with an insulin suspension (NPH or a premixed insulin), you should gently shake the pen to be sure the insulin is mixed before you inject. Pen needles should be removed after each use to prevent air from entering the cartridge and to prevent insulin from leaking out. There are many different pen needles available, in varying lengths and diameters. Although pens are very convenient, you can't mix multiple insulins with them. If you typically inject short- and long-acting insulin together, with a pen you'll need to give yourself two injections.

Pens v. syringes. Pens can offer more accurate dosing compared with syringes, and because you dial a mechanical device for the right dose and don't have to look at the syringe side, a pen provides more accurate dosing for anyone with vision problems.

WHEN TO TAKE INSULIN

Follow your doctor's advice about when to take your insulin, but typically you'd coordinate your insulin injection with when you want to eat. That's because the insulin should begin working in your body as your food is being absorbed, in order to avoid low blood sugar. For example, you would inject a rapid-acting insulin about 15 minutes before you eat, or right after you eat. Short-acting insulins such as regular insulin should be injected between a half hour to an hour before a meal. You can inject intermediate-acting insulins up to one hour before a meal.

Only long-acting insulins are not timed to a meal, because they last so long. Instead, ultralente is taken once or twice a day without regard to mealtimes. Lantus and Levemir are only administered once a day, at the same time each day (at times it maybe necessary to administer twice a day). However, if you're combining a long-acting insulin with a shorter-acting product, the shorter insulin still must be timed with mealtime.

There are several different standard dosing regiments for taking insulin, as listed below.

Multiple daily injection regimen. This plan involves at least three shots of insulin a day, which will give you good control of blood sugar. Basically, you inject longer-acting insulin plus shorter-acting insulin as needed. You might take a mixed injection in the morning, a shot before eating dinner, and an injection before bed. Alternatively, you could take one mixed shot before breakfast, one shot before lunch, and one before supper.

Two shots daily. In a "split schedule," you'd inject intermediate-acting insulin twice a day, the first about 30 minutes before breakfast (this one usually includes a larger chunk of the total insulin dose). You'd take the second shot about a half hour before dinner. Blood sugar would be checked before each meal, and again before bedtime.

In the "split mixed schedule," you take two shots of a mixture of short- or rapid-acting insulin and intermediate-acting insulin; the first shot is given about 30 minutes before breakfast, and the second about 30 minutes before dinner. The short-acting insulin is available for breakfast, and the intermediate insulin peaks after lunch, and in the same way, the mixed insulins in the second shot cover dinner and

Somogyi Effect

If you've had an untreated insulin reaction during the night, you may experience a sudden spike in blood sugar. The sudden increase is caused by the release of stress hormones in response to low blood sugar levels. People who experience high blood sugar levels in the morning may need to test their levels in the middle of the night. If blood sugar levels are falling or are already low, adjustments in evening snacks or insulin doses may be necessary. This condition is named after Dr. Michael Somogyi, the man who first discovered it.

early evening. You'll need to check your blood sugar about 45 minutes before each meal, plus extra checks during exercise or snacks.

The only problem with the two-shot method is that insulin from the second shot can peak at night, leading to low blood sugar when you're asleep. Your doctor can work with you if this is a problem.

STORING INSULIN

You should keep unopened bottles of insulin in the refrigerator until their expiration dates, but you can keep an opened bottle for up to 28 days. But because some types of insulin have different life spans, follow the manufacturer's directions on the label.

All insulins should look cloudy after you shake them (except regular, which should be clear). Do not use if the bottle looks frosted, if there are clumps of insulin, or the insulin stays at the bottom even after shaking.

COMING SOON: PAIN-FREE DIABETES CARE

Doctors expect that soon there will be an easier way to take insulin without having to use injections. Earlier ideas, such as insulin patches or pills, have not worked out, but new methods of giving insulin, such as inhaling it, are showing great promise for kids with both Type 1 and Type 2 diabetes. The inhaled insulin comes in a dry-powder delivery system similar to some asthma inhalers. When it hits the lungs, it's absorbed directly into the bloodstream, so that it takes effect faster than injected insulin does. Both ways of delivering insulin can be adjusted to accommodate meals, exercise, and so on. However, inhaled insulin isn't yet available. Long-term safety studies must first be completed.

In addition, new methods of testing blood sugar levels without having to prick the skin are being developed.

WHAT YOU NEED TO KNOW

- Medications to treat Type 2 diabetes are NOT pill forms of insulin, but a separate group of medications that include five classes of drugs: thiazolidinediones, biguanides, sulfonylureas, meglitinides, and alpha-glucosidase inhibitors.
- People with Type 1 diabetes need an insulin pump or insulin injections; people with Type 2 diabetes may need to use either medication or (much less often) insulin.
- Thiazolidinediones and metformin are insulin sensitizers typically prescribed first for Type 2 diabetes, which makes the body more sensitive to insulin.
- Sulfonylureas and meglitinides stimulate the insulin-producing cells in the pancreas (the beta cells) to produce more insulin, which should make the blood sugar level drop.
- Alpha-glucosidase inhibitors delay the absorption of carbohydrates in the small intestine and include Acarbose (Precose) and meglitol (Glyset).
- Different classes of diabetes drugs act in different ways, so you can combine two or more to get better blood sugar control.
- After taking oral medications for years, they may suddenly stop working. Doubling up on two different medications may be more effective if this happens.
- Exenatide (Byetta) is a newly approved injectable class of drugs called incretin mimetics for Type 2 diabetes and are usually prescribed for patients who haven't responded to metformin, a sulfonylurea, or a combination of metformin and a sulfonylurea.
- To help protect against heart and circulatory problems, your doctor may recommend a low daily dose of aspirin or a group of blood pressure drugs called ACE inhibitors that have been shown to protect the heart and the kidneys of people with diabetes.
- You'll need insulin if you have Type 1 diabetes and Type 2 diabetes, if other medications, in combination with diet and exercise changes, don't help lower your blood sugar.
- There are many varieties of insulin ranging from fast-acting to long-acting.

- Your diabetes medical management plan will outline the correct dosage, delivery system, and schedule for insulin administration.
- A coordinated combination of insulins is used to allow for adequate treatment of diabetes at meals, snacks, during periods of physical activity, and through the night.
- Most insulin today is synthetic human insulin, which is typically more quickly absorbed than animal insulin.
- Rapid-acting insulin (Humalog and Novolog) lasts for between three and five hours.
- Short-acting insulin (Humulin R, Novolin R, Velosulin human) is effective within 30 minutes to an hour, peaks in two to four hours, and lasts for six to eight hours.
- Intermediate-acting insulin includes NPH (Humulin N, Novolin N) and lente (Humulin L, Novolin L), both of which last for between 18 and 24 hours.
- Long-acting insulin include lantus, levemir, and ultralente (Humulin U); onset for ultralente is between 30 minutes and three hours, and is one to one-and-a-half hours for lantus and two hours for levemir.
- Because every person with diabetes has a slightly different reaction to insulin, it's important for you to know (by checking your blood sugar) how insulin affects *you*.
- The three most common ways to administer insulin are with a syringe, an insulin pen, or an insulin pump.
- Typically you coordinate your insulin injection with when you want to eat so the insulin can begin working in your body as your food is being absorbed, in order to avoid low blood sugar.
- You can inject insulin multiple times during the day (at least three) or on a twice-daily schedule.
- Keep unopened bottles of insulin in the refrigerator until their expiration date; an opened bottle at room temperature or in the fridge for 28 days.

9

Complications of Uncontrolled Diabetes

If you're a teenager with diabetes, the idea that some-day you might develop complications can seem like a remote possibility. So remote, in fact, that many teens don't consider it at all. It's true that the outlook today for teens with Type 1 or Type 2 diabetes is much brighter than in the past. Still, that doesn't mean that there aren't risks and complications, especially if your diabetes is in poor control. It's important for you to understand the future risks linked to diabetes, because taking care of your condition now can prevent many problems later in life.

The bottom line: People with Type 1 or Type 2 diabetes are at a much higher risk than healthy people for having problems with their eyes, kidneys, nerves, and blood vessels. Because of these serious risks, the American Diabetes Association recommends regular screenings to check for early signs of damage. The good news is that many of these side effects can be delayed or completely avoided as long as you carefully maintain good blood sugar control. You can reduce your risk of complications by learning as much as you can about your condition, controlling your blood sugar as well as you can, keeping your blood pressure and cholesterol levels under control, and having regular checkups.

HEART AND CIRCULATION PROBLEMS

The most serious complications of diabetes are heart disease and stroke, which occur twice as often among people with diabetes. Diabetes can affect the health of your veins and arteries, influencing the flow of blood throughout the entire body, but especially the veins in your heart and brain.

When sugar builds up in the blood of people with diabetes, it attaches to proteins in the blood vessels, making them thicker and less elastic. This makes it harder for blood to circulate. High levels of sugar in the blood also may make the fats in the blood stickier so that they attach to artery walls. In many ways like this, blood sugar can damage blood vessels, making them less able to dilate, and leading to blockage. This is called hardening of the arteries (atherosclerosis), and diabetes seems to make this process occur faster.

SYMPTOMS

If this hardening affects the coronary arteries leading to the heart, it can make it harder for the heart to pump and lead to chest pain. If the arteries become completely blocked, this can cause a heart attack; blocked arteries to the brain can cause a stroke. People with diabetes have two to four times the risk of developing heart disease or stroke than the general population. The risk of cardiovascular disease among people with diabetes is significant; more than 65 percent of deaths in diabetes patients are attributed to heart and vascular disease.

Blocked vessels in the legs can cause pain and interfere with circulation, making small cuts or infections less likely to heal. In extreme cases, this can lead to gangrene. Eventually, some diabetics have so much damage to their feet or lower legs that they must have a lower limb amputated.

HOW TO PREVENT DIABETES-RELATED CARDIOVASCULAR DISEASE

Just because you have diabetes doesn't mean that heart problems and stroke are inevitable. You can do a lot to prevent heart disease and stroke, starting right now. First, keep your blood sugar as close to normal as possible. If your doctor gives you an A1c test at least twice a year, this will tell you what your average blood sugar has been for the last couple of months. Aim for a number below 7.

Keep your blood pressure normal, below 130/80, if possible. Your doctor will check your blood pressure at every visit. At the same time, watch over your cholesterol and make sure it doesn't get too high. Have it checked at least once a year, and try to keep the LDL (bad) cholesterol below 100, and the HDL (good) cholesterol above

40 in men and above 50 in women. Triglycerides (another type of fat) should be less than 150.

Just because you have diabetes doesn't mean you should be afraid to exercise; don't make the mistake of sitting around on the couch or in front of your computer for hours at a time. Exercise is vital to your health; aim for at least 30 minutes of exercise most days. Ask your doctor what activities are best, but most people can certainly aim for a half-hour walk every day (or a 10-minute stroll after each meal).

If you have diabetes, you should already be watching your diet closely. Aim for heart-healthy foods high in fiber, with plenty of fruits and vegetables, and try to avoid as much as possible foods high in saturated fat or cholesterol. If you have Type 2 diabetes, make sure your weight is appropriate and lose weight if your doctor thinks this is a good idea. Being at a normal weight will really help to protect your heart.

Ask your doctor if taking a daily aspirin makes sense for you. Studies have shown that taking a low dose of aspirin every day can help reduce your risk of heart disease and stroke.

You also should take a microalbumin test to assess your risk for vascular disease. This test looks for small amounts of protein in the urine that can't be detected by routine urinanalysis, using specialized dipsticks or urine collections over a period of 12 to 24 hours. Persistent microalbumin over several repeated tests at different times suggests a higher risk for macrovascular disease.

EYE PROBLEMS

Diabetes blocks not just the major arteries, but also the tiniest of the minor blood vessels of the eyes and kidneys. These tiny blood vessels are crucial in maintaining the health of the retina. Eye damage can begin in as little as five years after diabetes is first diagnosed and often causes no symptoms in the beginning. Within 15 years of diagnosis of both Type 1 and Type 2 diabetes, many diabetics will have at least some damage to the retina. Diabetes is the leading cause of new cases of blindness in people ages 20 to 74. Each year, from 12,000 to 24,000 people lose their sight because of diabetes.

PREVENTING EYE PROBLEMS

The most important thing you can do to protect your eyes is to keep your blood sugar and blood pressure as normal as possible. Because the retina can be irreversibly damaged before you notice any change in vision, and because this damage is treatable if caught soon enough, the American Diabetes Association recommends yearly vision screening. As part of this exam, your eye doctor should dilate your eyes to inspect the back of your eye. The earlier you diagnose any eye problems and get the proper treatment, the easier it will be to prevent more serious problems.

TYPES OF EYE PROBLEMS

The high blood sugar and high blood pressure typical of diabetes can damage any of the four different parts of your eyes: the retina, the vitreous, the lens, and the optic nerve.

Retina. The lining at the back of your eye is called the retina. It senses light as it enters the eye. The retina is filled with tiny blood vessels that are vulnerable to damage in people with diabetes. The most common and potentially serious eye complication is called proliferative retinopathy, which occurs when blood vessels in the retina balloon out into pouches. This early stage does not affect vision, but it can progress as damaged blood vessels close off and new, weaker vessels take their place. As the blood vessels swell and weaken, they begin to get clogged with debris, and the trickle of blood slows down. At first, you may not notice any problems, but as the weakened blood vessels begin to break, blood leaks into the fluid behind the eye (called the vitreous). This leaking blood prevents light from reaching the retina, so you may start to see spots floating in your vision. Other people will experience almost total darkness. If the blood doesn't go away by itself, you'll need surgery to remove it.

After many years, the damaged blood vessels form scar tissue, which pulls the retina away from the back of the eye. This may cause floating spots, flashing lights, or areas of darkness. A detached retina is serious; untreated, it can result in diminished vision or blindness.

Vitreous. The vitreous is the squishy fluid that fills the back of your eye. When blood vessels in the eye are weakened by diabetes, they can break, allowing blood to leak into the vitreous. This prevents light from reaching the retina, significantly reducing vision. If this leaking blood doesn't get better on its own, a doctor can surgically remove the vitreous, replacing it with a clear solution.

Lens. Just like a sort of telescope, the lens at the front part of your eye focuses light on the back of your eye (the retina). People with diabetes are susceptible to cataracts, which look a bit like a film coating the lens of your eye, which should be clear. If you have cataracts, everything you see looks filmy.

Optic nerve. Your brain is a vital part of helping you to see and interpret vision; the optic nerve is the main nerve that connects your eyes and your brain. Some people with diabetes develop glaucoma, which begins when pressure starts to build up in the eye. Over time, this pressure damages the optic nerve, so that you lose sight from the sides of your eyes.

TREATMENT

Luckily, modern laser surgery can repair problems caused by retinal damage and prevent further loss of vision. Your eye doctor may suggest laser treatment to close off leaking blood vessels in the retina, which may stop blood and fluid from leaking into the vitreous, slowing the loss of vision.

If a lot of blood has leaked into the vitreous and your eyesight isn't good, your eye doctor might suggest a type of surgery called a vitrectomy. During a vitrectomy, the doctor removes blood and fluids from the vitreous of your eye, replacing it with fluid.

Cataracts can be removed during surgery, when a plastic lens replaces your clouded original lens. This plastic lens remains in your eye all the time. Glaucoma can be treated with special daily eye drops or laser surgery to lower the pressure in the eye.

KIDNEY DISEASE

Kidney disease (known medically as nephropathy) is a common complication of both types of diabetes and often ends in kidney failure. It can take many years to reach this state. Kidney damage rarely begins until you've had diabetes for between 15 to 25 years; if you manage to pass 25 years without any signs of kidney failure, your risk of kidney problems drops. Eventually, however, as many as 21 percent of everyone with diabetes will develop kidney disease, and it's the leading cause of kidney failure in this country. Type 1 diabetes is more likely to end in kidney failure (20 to 40 percent of people with Type 1 develop kidney failure by age 50), but between 1993 and 1997, more than 100,000 Americans with Type 2 diabetes also were treated for kidney failure.

Partly, race may put you at risk, although scientists don't know why. African Americans, American Indians, and Hispanic Americans develop diabetes and kidney failure at higher-than-average rates. Experts do know that high blood pressure and high blood sugar levels increase your risk of developing kidney failure. This is why the American Diabetes Association and the National Heart, Lung, and Blood Institute recommend that people with diabetes keep their blood pressure below 130/80 and their blood sugar levels as normal as possible.

Your kidneys are a pair of tiny bean-shaped organs in the abdomen that filter out impurities and waste products from your blood, excreting them as urine. They also control the level of some chemicals in the blood, such as salt, potassium, and water, which also influences blood pressure. If you have diabetes, your kidneys are especially vulnerable because the kidneys' very delicate blood vessels can be damaged. In fact, diabetes is the leading cause of end-stage kidney failure in the United States.

Kidney disease begins when the blood vessels in the kidney begin to leak, which allows protein from the blood to leak into urine. (It's this protein that doctors detect when they test for kidney function.) As blood vessels begin to collapse, the remaining blood vessels can't handle the work, and the kidney may fail. If the disease progresses, the patient may need either to go on dialysis or receive a kidney transplant. Even if you can control your blood sugar with drugs and diet, diabetes can still lead to kidney failure. However, most people with diabetes don't develop kidney problems severe enough to cause kidney failure.

PREVENTING KIDNEY PROBLEMS

Just because you have diabetes doesn't mean that kidney disease is inevitable. Since the mid-1990s, about a third fewer Americans with diabetes are developing kidney failure. In fact, research has found that people with Type 1 diabetes who improve their blood sugar control can either delay or prevent the development of kidney disease. The key is keeping your blood sugar under control, making sure your blood pressure is normal, and getting regular health screens. The American Diabetes Association recommends screening for protein in the urine every year starting when you are first diagnosed with Type 2 diabetes or five years after the diagnosis in Type 1.

Microalbumin test. You can monitor your risk for diabetic nephropathy by taking the microalbumin test. This test looks at small amounts of protein in the urine that can't be detected by routine urinanalysis. Specialized dipsticks, or urine collections over a period of 12 to 24 hours, are used to measure the amount of microalbumin. If there is persistent microalbumin over several repeated tests at different times, there is a higher risk of diabetic nephropathy.

SYMPTOMS OF KIDNEY DAMAGE

As you start to develop kidney disease, small amounts of a blood protein called albumin will begin to spill over into your urine. As kidney disease gets worse, more albumin leaks into the urine, and your kidney's function begins to falter. As your kidneys have more trouble filtering wastes from your blood, they build up; creatinine is one waste product that doctors can measure in your blood to assess how poorly your kidneys are doing. As kidney damage continues, your blood pressure often will rise.

TREATMENT OF KIDNEY DAMAGE

If you have either Type 1 or Type 2 diabetes and you're only in the early stages of kidney problems, intensive management of your blood sugar can help prevent further damage. Keeping your blood sugar levels close to normal means you'll need to test your blood sugar often, take insulin often throughout the day depending on diet and exercise (if you have Type 1), follow a healthy diet and exercise plan, and stay in close contact with your doctor. Some patients find it easiest to use an insulin pump throughout the day.

There are other things you can do to try to keep your kidneys from further deterioration. Blood pressure drugs (ACE inhibitors and angiotensin receptor blockers [ARB]) can slow the progression of kidney disease. Many people require two or more drugs to control their blood pressure. A diuretic drug also is useful. Beta blockers, calcium channel blockers, and other blood pressure drugs may also be needed.

Diet is also important in controlling diabetes-related kidney disease. Eating too much protein may be harmful, so you should avoid high-protein diets. If your kidneys are already impaired, eating less protein may help delay kidney failure.

Once your kidneys fail, you must either undergo dialysis to help filter your blood or have a kidney transplant. Both transplants and dialysis work well in the short run, although other complications are more common than in people without diabetes, because of other diabetic-related problems of heart, nerve, and eye damage.

NERVE DAMAGE

Eventually, poorly controlled diabetes can damage the nerves throughout the body, causing numbness or even pain and weakness in the arms, hands, feet, and legs. Nerve damage also can affect your digestive tract, heart, and sex organs. If you have diabetes, you can develop problems with your nerves at any time, but the longer you have diabetes, the higher your risk. About half of everybody with diabetes has at least some nerve damage, although there may not be any symptoms at first. The biggest risk for nerve damage, however, doesn't occur until you've had diabetes for at least 25 years.

Diabetes-related nerve damage affects the nerves that let you sense temperature, pressure, texture, or pain. The real problem begins when numbness allows injuries to the foot to go unnoticed. For this reason, the American Diabetes Association recommends that everybody with diabetes have a thorough foot exam every year. You're also more likely to have nerve problems if you haven't been able to control your blood sugar, if you have very high cholesterol and blood pressure, if you're overweight, and if you're over age 40. The risk of a leg amputation is 15 to 40 times greater for a person with diabetes. Each year, more than 82,000 amputations are performed on people with diabetes.

Doctors aren't sure exactly what leads to the nerve damage, but they think it must be some combination of high blood sugar, high cholesterol and blood pressure, genetics, autoimmune factors, damaged blood vessels carrying oxygen to nerves, and lifestyle (such as smoking or drinking too much).

PREVENTING NERVE DAMAGE

It's a lot easier to prevent nerve damage than it is to treat it once it occurs. The best way to prevent neuropathy is to keep your blood sugar level as close to normal as you can, which will protect the nerves throughout your body. In addition, you should try to avoid getting cuts and sores, bunions, or calluses on your feet. You should check your feet, toes, and toenails every day, and make sure your shoes and socks fit well. You need to check your feet because you may have less feeling and may not notice cuts or foot problems right away.

TYPES OF NERVE DAMAGE

Doctors have some fancy terms to describe the different types of nerve damage that a person with diabetes may experience. Nerve disease (neuropathies) may either be peripheral, autonomic, proximal, or focal. People with diabetes also tend to develop compressed nerves. You've probably heard of carpal tunnel syndrome—that's a condition in which a compressed nerve causes numbness and tingling, weakness, or pain in the hand.

Peripheral neuropathy. This problem causes numbness, prickling, or tingling or sharp pain or cramps in the toes, feet, legs, hands, arms, and fingers, or wasting of your feet or hands. There may be extreme sensitivity to touch and a loss of balance and coordination. Problems normally appear with the feet and legs before the hands and arms. People with peripheral neuropathy may notice weakened muscles, especially at the ankle, so that walking becomes more difficult. Hammertoes and the collapse of the midfoot may occur. Because the foot may be numb, blisters and sores may develop because pressure is unnoticed.

Once foot injuries develop, they must be treated immediately or infection may spread to the bone; at that point, the foot may have to be amputated. Half of all such amputations could probably be prevented if minor problems were treated in time.

Autonomic neuropathy. If you have changes in your digestion, bowel, or bladder function, sexual response, or perspiration, you may have developed autonomic neuropathy, which affects the nerves that serve the heart and control blood pressure, the digestive system, the urinary tract, the sex organs, the sweat glands, and the eyes.

Autonomic neuropathy most often affects the organs that control urination and sexual function. This means you might have trouble emptying the bladder completely, leading to urinary tract infections. You may experience urinary incontinence, because you can't sense when the bladder is full or control the muscles that release urine.

Autonomic neuropathy also can make it difficult to notice low blood sugar, since the condition can interfere with the symptoms of hypoglycemia (such as sweating or heart palpitations).

Damage to nerves in the cardiovascular system interferes with the body's ability to adjust blood pressure and heart rate. This means that when you stand up quickly, your blood pressure may plummet, making you feel dizzy.

You may experience constipation as a result of nerve damage to the digestive system, or you may have nausea and vomiting, bloating, and loss of appetite because the stomach empties too slowly. Swallowing may be more difficult as a result of nerve damage to the esophagus. You may lose weight because of problems with the digestive system.

You may experience profuse sweating at night or while you're eating, because nerve damage prevents the sweat glands from working properly.

Proximal neuropathy. Pain in the thighs, hips, or buttocks may be due to a type of nerve damage called proximal neuropathy, which usually begins on one side of the body. This is more common with Type 2 diabetes. Proximal neuropathy also causes leg weakness, so that it's hard to stand up from a sitting position. People with this problem usually need to be treated for weakness or pain, and the length of the recovery period varies.

Focal neuropathy. Once in a while, nerve damage from diabetes causes a sudden weakness of one nerve, or a group of nerves, causing muscle weakness or pain. Any nerve in the body may be affected, but mostly this problem affects the eyes, facial muscles, ears, pelvis and lower back, thighs, and abdomen. It tends to appear in older people, but it also tends to get better by itself and doesn't usually cause any permanent damage.

DIAGNOSING NERVE DAMAGE

Your doctor can diagnose nerve damage by checking your symptoms and giving you a physical exam, checking your blood pressure and heart rate, muscle strength, and reflexes. The doctor will also want to see how sensitive you are to position, vibration, temperature, and light touch.

In addition, a comprehensive foot exam will reveal any problems with skin, circulation, or sensation. To assess how much feeling you have in the foot, your doctor will touch your feet with a type of hairbrush bristle. If you can't feel any pressure, you're at risk of foot sores. Your doctor also may check your reflexes and see how well you can perceive vibration.

The health of your nerves can be assessed with nerve conduction studies, which check for slower or weaker nerve impulses in the arms and legs. At the same time, your doctor may perform an electromyography (EMG) test to assess how well muscles respond to electrical signals transmitted by nearby nerves.

Your doctor may want to test whether you have lost any sensation or whether your nerves are unusually irritable with a quantitative sensory test (QST). The doctor will be looking at your response to pressure, vibration, and temperature to check for possible nerve damage.

Ultrasound tests of the bladder and urinary tract can reveal whether there are any irregularities and whether the bladder empties completely after urination.

TREATING NERVE DAMAGE

Once your nerves are damaged, your first order of business is to get your blood sugar back to normal with careful meal plans, exercise, and medication so you can prevent any further damage. Sometimes symptoms get a little worse when you first get blood sugar back to normal, but eventually normal blood sugar will ease symptoms. And if you can keep your blood sugar under control, you may prevent more problems later.

Foot care. Since the biggest problem of nerve disease is foot problems, anyone with diabetes needs to take particular care of their feet. First, be sure to keep your feet clean, washing them each day with warm (not hot) water and mild soap, followed by a soft towel dry. Each day, check your feet and toes for cuts, blisters, redness, swelling, calluses, or other problems. Slather lotion on your feet (but avoid the areas in between your toes). After a bath or shower, gently file any corns or calluses you may have with a pumice stone. As needed, cut your toenails and file the edges with an emery board. Don't go barefoot; always wear thick, soft socks and shoes or slippers to protect your feet. Make sure your shoes are roomy enough so that your toes can wiggle. Before putting your shoes on, make sure there are no tears, sharp edges, or objects inside that might injure your feet.

Easing pain. Neuropathies often may cause irritating pain, burning, tingling, or numbness. You can ease this discomfort with aspirin, acetaminophen, or nonsteroidal anti-inflammatory drugs (NSAIDs) such as ibuprofen (Motrin or Advil). However, if you also have kidney disease, you should use NSAIDs only with your doctor's advice. Alternatively, you might try a topical cream called capsaicin. Pain clinics have often recommended tricyclic antidepressant medications such as amitriptyline, imipramine, and nortriptyline, or anticonvulsant medications such as carbamazepine or gabapentin to ease pain. Codeine may be prescribed for a short time to relieve severe pain. Other pain treatments include a transcutaneous electronic nerve stimulation (TENS) device, which blocks pain signals by using spurts of electricity. Hypnosis, relaxation training, biofeedback, and acupuncture also may be effective.

Stomach problems. To relieve mild symptoms of indigestion, nausea, or vomiting, try eating smaller, more frequent meals, while avoiding fats and eating less fiber. For severe symptoms, your doctor may prescribe erythromycin or metoclopramide to speed digestion and help relieve nausea or other drugs to help regulate digestion or reduce stomach acid secretion. Tetracycline may ease diarrhea or other bowel problems.

Dizziness and weakness. Sitting or standing slowly can help prevent the dizziness linked to blood pressure and circulation problems. Raising the head of the bed or wearing elastic stockings also may help. Some people may benefit from eating more salt, and some may try high blood pressure medications. Physical therapy can help when muscle weakness or loss of coordination is a problem.

Urinary problems. Antibiotics are used to treat urinary tract infections, and drinking plenty of fluids (especially cranberry juice) will help prevent another infection.

DOUBLE DIABETES

You probably thought things were quite bad enough when you were diagnosed with diabetes, but some kids are surprised to learn that they have not one, but *two* forms of the disease. That's what happened to Connie, who was diagnosed with Type 1 diabetes at age 5 and coped for years with blood sugar tests, insulin administration, and detailed meal plans. But when she entered her early teens, she started gaining weight. Within a few years, she needed more and more insulin, which signaled developing insulin resistance. Doctors are calling this new phenomenon double diabetes, meaning that patients (often young people) are developing both Type 1 *and* Type 2 diabetes. (Other names for double diabetes are atypical diabetes, diabetes 1½, or Type 3 diabetes.) Sometimes, it occurs when kids who must give themselves insulin injections because they have Type 1 diabetes then gain weight and develop Type 2 diabetes because their bodies have become insulin resistant. Sometimes, a kid with Type 2 diabetes symptoms doesn't respond to diet, exercise, and medication regimen. Further tests reveal that he or she is developing the insulin-dependent form of the disease. Other kids don't really fall clearly in one category or the other.

It's important to correctly diagnose the type of diabetes, however, because different types require different treatments. That's why doctors get frustrated when a teenager doesn't have a clear-cut

Mauriac Syndrome

This rare condition occurs in children with Type 1 diabetes as a result of chronic poor blood sugar control. It causes obesity, dwarfism, and an enlarged liver caused by excessive glycogen deposits. Children diagnosed with this syndrome typically have a history of repeated hospitalizations for ketoacidosis. This syndrome is seldom seen today because of proper treatment with adequate food and insulin.

case of diabetes. While the experts haven't been able to come up with statistics about this diabetes mixture, some believe as many as one-fourth of kids with Type 1 diabetes are also overweight and have Type 2 symptoms. Researchers believe that many children with Type 2 diabetes have antibodies that suggest they may be developing Type 1.

Doctors aren't sure why this double diabetes occurs, but they do know that whatever causes it, having both types of diabetes certainly complicates treatment. Yet exactly what sort of treatment is required isn't clear either. Because of this, doctors are emphasizing prevention. If you have Type 2 diabetes, you'll be encouraged to lose weight.

WHAT YOU NEED TO KNOW

- People with Type 1 or Type 2 diabetes are at a much higher risk than healthy people for having problems with their eyes, kidneys, nerves, and blood vessels.
- Diabetes complications can be avoided by controlling blood sugar, keeping blood pressure and cholesterol levels under control, and having regular checkups.
- The most serious complications of diabetes are heart disease and stroke, which occur twice as often to people with diabetes.
- Diabetes can affect the health of your veins and arteries, influencing the flow of blood throughout the entire body, but especially the veins in your heart and brain.
- Blocked vessels in the legs can cause pain, interfere with circulation, and make small cuts or infections less likely to heal; eventually this can lead to gangrene.
- Diabetes blocks tiny blood vessels of the eyes, leading to retinal damage; diabetes is the leading cause of new cases of blindness in people ages 20 to 74.
- People with diabetes are also susceptible to cataracts and glaucoma.
- After many years, patients with diabetes may develop kidney disease that may end in kidney failure.
- Keeping blood sugar under control can delay or prevent the development of kidney disease and many other complications of diabetes.
- Poorly controlled diabetes can damage nerves, causing numbness or even pain and weakness in the arms, hands, feet, and legs and affecting the digestive tract, heart, and sex organs. The longer you have diabetes, the higher the risk.

- Peripheral neuropathy causes numbness, prickling or tingling, or sharp pain or cramps in the toes, feet, legs, hands, arms, and fingers, with extreme sensitivity to touch, and a loss of balance and coordination.
- Autonomic neuropathy affects the nerves affecting the heart, blood pressure, the digestive system, the urinary tract, the sex organs, the sweat glands, and the eyes, leading to changes in digestion, bowel or bladder function, sexual response, or perspiration.
- Proximal neuropathy causes pain in the thighs, hips, or buttocks, which usually begins on one side of the body.
- Focal neuropathy affects one nerve, or a group of nerves, causing muscle weakness or pain, primarily in the eyes, facial muscles, ears, pelvis and lower back, thighs, and abdomen.
- Nerve damage can be diagnosed with nerve conduction studies or an electromyography (EMG) test to assess how well muscles respond to electrical signals transmitted by nearby nerves.
- A quantitative sensory test (QST) assesses the loss of any sensation or nerve irritability.
- Anyone with diabetes must take particular care of their feet since the biggest problem of nerve disease is foot problems.
- Double diabetes occurs when patients (often young people) develop both Type 1 *and* Type 2 diabetes. (Other names for double diabetes are atypical diabetes, diabetes 1½, or Type 3 diabetes.)

10

Helping Others Cope with Diabetes

Liz was a 16-year-old sophomore when her best friend, Steffi, was diagnosed with Type 2 diabetes. Because her condition was severe, Steffi needed to inject insulin as well as think constantly about her diet and exercise. Liz wanted to be supportive, but she didn't quite know what to say, and she felt uncomfortable eating snacks in front of Steffi. The two used to stop by the snack machine on their way to study hall. Now Liz doesn't know what to do—would it be rude to grab a soda or a chocolate bar in front of her, knowing that Steffi can't have one?

TALKING ABOUT DIABETES

If you know someone who has just been diagnosed with diabetes, this scenario probably sounds pretty familiar. Some kids wonder whether they should bring up the diagnosis or whether it's kinder not to say anything at all. But what if the person *wants* to talk about it?

Probably the best rule to keep in mind is that if you care about the person, that will come through whatever you say or do. If the person has told you of the diagnosis or knows you know about it, there's certainly nothing wrong with asking how the person feels and are they okay. If the person wants to talk about it, they will. If not, they'll probably let you know that too. Take your lead from the way your friend or family member behaves.

Diabetes will be a big part of your friend's life, but so are you. Never forget that! The problem with having a chronic health problem is that many people will suddenly treat the person with diabetes as if she's fragile or "sick," rather than like a normal person. Work hard to treat your friend just the way you always have.

PITFALLS TO AVOID

What you want to avoid is turning into the Diet Police, commenting on anything the person chooses to eat or drink. It's *not* okay to say "Hey, should you be eating that? It's covered with chocolate!" Let your friend take responsibility for her condition—you don't have to.

The person probably also doesn't want to hear your thoughts on the latest diabetes article you read on the Internet. Rest assured that your friend probably hears expert advice from dozens of people all the time, such as how Great-Aunt Sue or Grandma managed *her* diabetes. Even worse are the horror stories: "My cousin Debbie used to date a guy who went blind because he didn't take care of his diabetes." First of all, nobody needs to hear horror stories like this, and second, the implied criticism—"it was his fault he went blind"—is insensitive. If your friend has been diagnosed, you can be sure his or her diabetes educator has thoroughly explained the condition, including the complications that can occur.

What you *can* do is simply be supportive and listen. Diabetes can be a pain sometimes, especially during adolescence. Your friend may get really frustrated with having to take pills, worry about diet, or handle injections. You might say something like: "Hey, I can't imagine how rough this must be for you. You can talk to me about it anytime—that's what friends are for."

IF YOUR FRIEND IS DEPRESSED OR ALOOF

At first, some kids feel overwhelmed with the diagnosis and worry so much about being different that they go too far in the opposite direction, declining any support at all. Others worry about seeming needy, whiney, or a burden. Letting your friend know you're ready to be a support can be invaluable.

This doesn't mean, however, that you have to turn into a doormat. If you feel as if the friendship is turning into a one-way pity party, you need to speak up. If your friend only uses you to dump all his or her negative feelings, eventually the friendship will suffer if you don't point out what's happening. It could be that your friend is so busy concentrating on the new diagnosis that he or she doesn't realize its impact on you.

If your friend is becoming seriously depressed, this is a situation that will require more than a sympathetic ear. No matter how caring you may be, you're just not trained or equipped to pull your friend out of the depths of a clinical depression. If you think that's what is happening, try to talk to your friend and suggest a consultation with the school psychologist or counselor. If your friend resists and you're really worried, you might want to drop a confidential word to the school nurse, counselor, trusted teacher, or principal. This isn't "ratting" on a friend. Depression is a serious medical illness that can be successfully treated, but only if it's first recognized.

TIPS FOR SOCIAL EVENTS

At some point after the diagnosis, you might want to invite your friend over to your house for a sleepover or just to hang out. It's perfectly okay to ask if your friend has any specific food or beverage needs before he comes over. You can ask your parents to stock up on diet soda or some healthy snacks. You should also ask your friend if it matters what *time* you eat. If you're planning a party, remember your friend with diabetes, and don't limit the food to high-sugar, high-carb contents. Keep some fresh fruit, diet drinks, and healthy low-fat food around.

Above all, if your friend declines any food or sidesteps a second helping, smile and accept it gracefully. And should your mom or dad forget and ask your friend twice if she wants a sugary dessert, don't make a big announcement at the table: "Mom! Don't you remember? Sara has diabetes!" First of all, drawing attention to a guest's problem in this way is just bad manners. It's bound to make your friend feel uncomfortable.

IF YOUR SIBLING HAS DIABETES

If your brother or sister is diagnosed with diabetes, that will usually mean lots of changes in his or her daily life, especially if it's Type 1 diabetes. For example, your brother or sister may have to take lots of insulin shots at odd times and perhaps have an occasional low blood sugar emergency. Timing of your family meals will probably become a lot more strict.

Having a chronic illness can be really difficult, so don't be surprised if your sister or brother gets frustrated, angry, or upset about having to do things differently and sometimes missing out on things. Nobody likes to feel different, especially kids. It may be particularly hard for your sibling to see you able to do the things you always do, because that will be a reminder of the new restrictions in his or her

Be a Pen Pal with a Diabetes Sibling

You might enjoy writing to someone else who has a brother or sister with diabetes. To find a pen pal in this situation, write to the Family & Friend Pen Pal Bulletin Board at the Web site for the Juvenile Diabetes Research Foundation International: http://kids.jdrf.org/index.cfm?fuseaction=penpals.home.

life. The more you can try to be understanding and treat your brother or sister the same as you always did, the better.

Having diabetes can feel like a pretty big deal, so be prepared to help your sibling cope with lots of uncomfortable feelings, such as fear, sadness, hopelessness, or loneliness. Try your best to be supportive, but remember your sib may just need some time to adjust to all these changes.

Don't be surprised if *you* have some uncomfortable feelings too. It's perfectly normal to have a jumble of conflicting feelings, including sorrow and sympathy for your brother or sister, right along with anger or jealousy for all the extra time your parents are giving to someone else. Maybe you get angry because your mom says you can't have ice cream or cake in the house anymore, because it's too much of a temptation for your little brother or sister. Maybe you feel like the other adults who come to the house all cluster around your diabetic sibling, and you get left out in the cold. All of those emotions are normal. But just because you have those feelings doesn't mean you have to act on them. You might want to talk about how you're feeling with your parents or with your sibling's diabetes educator; it's certainly something the experts are very familiar with! Don't be afraid to ask your parents for help in working this out. This may be hard to believe right now, but eventually diabetes can bring the family closer.

HOW TO RECOGNIZE A DIABETIC EMERGENCY

It may never happen, but if a family member or close friend has diabetes, it's helpful to know how to recognize the signs of very low or

Symptoms of a Diabetic Emergency

First signs of hypoglycemia:

- anxiety
- feeling cold
- hunger
- rapid heartbeat
- shakiness
- sudden sweating

As blood sugar levels continue to drop, symptoms worsen:

- blurry vision
- concentration problems
- confusion

very high blood sugar and to know how to treat it. Ask ahead of time where your friend keeps emergency sugar tablets or a quick sugar source.

Treating mild/moderate hypoglycemia. Remember that mild hypoglycemia is normally more unpleasant than anything else. But make sure your friend doesn't ignore it; if it's not treated promptly, hypoglycemia can lead to unconsciousness and convulsions. In rare cases, it can be life threatening.

If your friend is experiencing any symptoms of low blood sugar, never leave him or her alone. As soon as you realize what is happening, make sure the person eats or drinks one of the following types of quick-acting sugar:

- disorientation
- dizziness
- headache
- irritability
- lethargy
- pallor
- personality changes (belligerence, anger, or insisting there's nothing wrong)
- sleepiness
- slurred speech
- uncoordination
- weakness

- four ounces of fruit juice
- six ounces of *non-diet* soda
- six jelly beans, 10 gumdrops, or eight Life Savers
- six saltines
- two tablespoons of raisins
- four packets of granulated sugar
- a tablespoon of honey
- three or four glucose tablets
- three teaspoons (or three-fourths of a tube) of glucose gel

If all you happen to have with you is a chocolate bar, give that. Any carb is better than nothing.

Severe Symptoms

- inability to swallow
- seizures or jerking movements
- convulsions
- unconsciousness
- unresponsiveness
- coma

Severe hypoglycemia. Severe hypoglycemia is rare and can usually be prevented with prompt treatment when you first detect signs of low blood sugar. If you notice any of the following symptoms, you must get help for your friend right away.

In this situation, **never give your friend anything to eat or drink or put anything in your friend's mouth**—it could cause choking. Instead, roll the unconscious or convulsing person on the side to prevent choking. A trained person should then administer a glucagon injection. If there is no such person around, call for emergency medical assistance *immediately.*

WHAT YOU NEED TO KNOW

- Treat your friend or sibling with diabetes normally and be as supportive as you can.
- Avoid giving diet advice or discussing diabetes horror stories.
- If your friend is depressed, be supportive and get help if the depression seems severe.
- Have healthy snacks and diet soda on hand when a diabetic friend comes over, but don't call undue attention to the condition in public.
- Having a sibling with diabetes means you'll need to be supportive, but don't be surprised if you also experience some uncomfortable feelings yourself.

11

Paying for Care

Diabetes is a chronic condition, which means that you'll probably need continuing medical care for the rest of your life. People who have diabetes spend about $13,243 a year on health care expenses, according to the American Diabetes Association in 2002. That's why many people who have diabetes need help paying some of the bills.

Paying doctor bills is probably something you leave up to your parents, but if money is tight in your family, you're probably aware of the burden of health care costs. Diabetes medication and supplies can be expensive, and insurance premiums can be very high, making it tough on families. Many families find themselves in the uncomfortable position of making too much money to qualify for Medicaid coverage, but not enough to pay for your doctor visits and medication.

Fortunately, there are ways to get the care you might need. A variety of governmental and nongovernmental programs exist to help, depending on whether you qualify.

INSURANCE

If your family has medical insurance, the cost of your supplies and medications should be covered, although not all plans cover all types of medications.

If your family is currently without health insurance, the State Children's Health Insurance Program (SCHIP) provides free or low-cost health insurance for children. All 50 states have a health insurance

Low-Cost Health Care Clinics

The federal Bureau of Primary Health Care within the Health Resources and Services Administration (HRSA) has a nationwide network of community-based health care centers that provide primary health care services at little or no cost. For information, visit: http://www.ask.hrsa.gov/pc.

program for infants, children, and teens available to working families, including families that include individuals with a variety of immigration status. For little or no cost, this insurance pays for doctor visits, prescription medicines, hospitalizations, and much more. Kids who don't currently have health insurance are likely to be eligible, even if their parents are working. States have different eligibility rules, but in most states, uninsured children 18 years old and younger whose families earn up to $34,100 a year (for a family of four) are eligible. You can find details about SCHIP at: http://www.insurekidsnow.gov.

MEDICAID

Medicaid is a state-run public health program that covers medical care and transportation for people who live in poverty and earn less than the program's maximum income limit. States are required to cover a core set of benefits, including hospital, outpatient, doctor services, and home health services. Unfortunately, some states have already enacted, or are thinking about enacting, cuts to the program that cover durable medical equipment, including test strips, meters, and syringes. And some states don't cover prescription drugs, including insulin and oral medications. To find out exactly what your state does cover, you can visit the Medicaid Site for Consumer Information at http://www.cms.hhs.gov/MedicaidGenInfo.

More information about eligibility requirements is available at local welfare and medical assistance offices. Your parents can check with your state Medicaid office to see exactly what's covered where you live and what the income limits are. You also can find information about Medicaid at http://www.CMS.gov.

HOSPITAL CARE

Hospitals and other health care facilities participating in HRSA's Hill-Burton Program provide free and low-cost services to eligible individuals. To find a list of participating facilities, click on this Web site: http://www.hrsa.gov/hillburton/hillburtonfacilities.htm.

MEDICATION COSTS

Many medications and supplies used to manage diabetes are expensive, but even if your family's insurance doesn't cover drugs, or if your family doesn't have insurance at all, you can still get the supplies you need. Drug companies give free samples of their drugs to doctors; many physicians will offer these samples to you free if you can't afford them. If your doctor doesn't offer, ask about whether any samples are available.

In addition, most drug companies also offer free medications to patients who can't afford them. These special programs, usually called patient assistance programs or indigent drug programs, require a doctor's consent, proof of financial status, and proof that your family has no health insurance or prescription drug benefits.

The Partnership for Prescription Assistance provides information about public and private patient assistance programs, which help low-income, uninsured patients get free or nearly free brand-name medicines. The national program, which is sponsored by America's pharmaceutical research companies to help patients in need access prescription medicines, is the largest private effort in the country helping to provide care to needy patients. You can find more information about the program by visiting their Web site at: https://www.pparx.org/Intro.php.

Patient assistance programs. Individual drug companies often list their programs online, but to make things easier, you can visit several Web sites (listed below) that have gathered information about many patient assistance programs providing free prescription medications to eligible participants.

NAMI Prescription Drug Patient Assistance Programs
http://www.nami.org/helpline/freemed.htm

NeedyMeds program
http://www.needymeds.com

RxOutreach
http://www.rxassist.org

The Medicine Program
http://www.themedicineprogram.com

Partnership for Prescription Assistance
https://www.pparx.org/Intro.php

Prescription Drug Assistance Programs
http://www.phrma.org.

Canadian medications. Many people save money by ordering their medications from Canada, a move that troubles the U.S. government, but which consumer advocates insist makes economic sense. If your parents are interested in this alternative, try to find a reputable Web site. Good choices include programs provided by several states for their residents to buy medications from Canada:

- **Illinois, Vermont, Wisconsin, Missouri, Kansas:** If you live in any of these states, you can participate in I-SaveRx, a simple mail-order pharmacy program that can save you money. The program was developed by the governor of Illinois to provide mail-order access to lower cost prescription drugs from Canada, the United Kingdom, and Ireland. You can participate if you live in Illinois, Vermont, Wisconsin, Missouri, and Kansas. Contact: http://www.i-saverx.net.
- **Minnesota:** The governor has set up a Web site to help residents find less expensive drugs by buying from the United Kingdom. Contact: Minnesota RxConnect at: http://www.state.mn.us/portal/mn/jsp/home.do?agency=Rx.
- **North Dakota:** This state's Web page on Canadian drugs offers detailed explanations and links to Web sites to help you import medications. Visit: http://www.governor.state.nd.us/prescription-drug.html.

WHAT YOU NEED TO KNOW

- Uninsured children of working parents can obtain free or low-cost health insurance from the State Children's Health Insurance Program (SCHIP) available in all 50 states.
- Medicaid is a state-run public health program that covers medical care and transportation for people with diabetes who live in poverty and earn less than the program's maximum income limit, but not all states cover all medications.

- Hospitals and other health care facilities participating in HRSA's Hill-Burton Program provide free and low-cost services to eligible individuals.
- Drug companies give free samples of their drugs to doctors; many physicians will offer these samples to you free if you can't afford them.
- The Partnership for Prescription Assistance provides information about public and private patient assistance programs, which help low-income, uninsured patients get free or nearly free brand-name medicines.
- Individual drug companies often provide free prescription medications to eligible participants, with details online.

APPENDIX

Associations and Support Groups

American Academy of Family Physicians (AAFP)
11400 Tomahawk Creek Parkway
Leawood, KS 66211
(913) 906-6000
http://www.aafp.org
The AAFP is the national member organization of family doctors. Its Web site includes articles about the link between obesity and diabetes in young people and how to help children lose weight.

American Academy of Pediatrics (AAP)
141 Northwest Point Boulevard
Elk Grove Village, IL 60007-1098
(847) 434-4000
http://www.aap.org
The AAP is a professional organization committed to physical, mental, and social health and well-being for all infants, children, adolescents, and young adults.

American Association of Diabetes Educators (AADE)
100 West Monroe Street, Suite 400
Chicago, IL 60603
(800) TEAM-UP4 or (800) 832-6874
http://www.aadenet.org
The AADE is a multidisciplinary organization for health professionals who provide diabetes education and care. The AADE Web site provides diabetes links, including information about diabetes in children and adolescents.

American Council on Exercise (ACE)
4851 Paramount Drive
San Diego, CA 92123
(858) 535-8227

http://www.acefitness.org
The ACE is a nonprofit organization that promotes active, healthy lifestyles and their positive effects on the mind, body, and spirit.

American Diabetes Association (ADA)
1701 North Beauregard Street
Alexandria, VA 22311
(800) 342-2383
http://www.diabetes.org
The ADA's mission is to prevent and cure diabetes and improve the lives of people with diabetes. Founded in 1940, the association conducts programs in all 50 states and the District of Columbia, reaching hundreds of communities across the country. The ADA is a nonprofit organization that provides diabetes research, information, and advocacy. The association offers a variety of programs focused on young people with diabetes.

American Dietetic Association (ADA)
120 South Riverside Plaza, Suite 2000
Chicago, IL 60606-6995
(800) 877-1600
(800) 366-1655 (consumer referral)
http://www.eatright.org
The ADA is a member organization for registered dieticians and registered technicians representing special interests, including public health, sports nutrition, medical nutrition therapy, diet counseling for weight control, cholesterol reduction, and diabetes. More than 5,000 dieticians now belong to the ADA's specialty group on Diabetes Care and Education.

American Medical Association (AMA)
Science, Quality and Public Health Group
515 N. State Street
Chicago, IL 60610
(312) 464-4908
The AMA is the nation's leader in promoting professionalism in medicine and setting standards for medical education, practice, and ethics. As the largest physician membership organization in the United States, the AMA is at the forefront of every major development in medicine and promotes the art and science of medicine and the betterment of public health.

American Podiatric Medical Association (APMA)
9312 Old Georgetown Road
Bethesda, MD 20814-1698
(800) 366-8227 (toll-free)
(301) 571-9200
askapma@apma.org
http://www.apma.org
The professional organization representing the nation's podiatrists, with lots of information about foot care on the Web site. The APMA represents about 80 percent of the podiatrists in the country.

American School Health Association (ASHA)
Route 43, P.O. Box 708
Kent, OH 44240
(330) 678-1601
http://www.ashaweb.org
The mission of the ASHA is to promote and improve the well-being of children and youth by supporting comprehensive school health programs. In addition to a journal, the association produces a book for school nurses and families on managing school-age children with chronic health conditions.

American Urological Association (AUA)
1000 Corporate Boulevard
Linthicum, MD 21090
(866) 746-4282 (toll-free)
(410) 689-3700
http://www.urologyhealth.org
The largest professional association for the advancement of urologic patient care, providing the latest information on research and practices in urology, including the relationship of diabetes to urologic problems. The AUA pursues its mission of fostering the highest standards of urologic care by providing a wide range of services—including publications, research, the annual meeting, and continuing medical education.

Barbara Davis Center for Childhood Diabetes
4200 East Ninth Avenue
Box B-140
Denver, CO 80262
(303) 315-8796
http://www.barbaradaviscenter.org

The Barbara Davis Center for Childhood Diabetes is the largest diabetes and endocrine care program in Colorado with unique facilities and resources for clinicians, clinical researchers, and basic biomedical scientists working to help patients with Type 1 diabetes. The center provides state-of-the-art clinical diabetes care to a majority of children and many adults within the Rocky Mountain region.

Centers for Disease Control and Prevention (CDC)
4770 Buford Highway, NE
Atlanta, GA 30341
(800) 311-3435
http://www.cdc.gov
The CDC serves as the nation's focal point for developing and applying disease prevention and control, environmental health, and health promotion and education activities designed to improve the health of the people of the United States. CDC divisions with special relevance to diabetes in students include the Division of Diabetes Translation, the Division of Nutrition and Physical Activity, and the Division of Adolescent and School Health.

CDC Division of Adolescent and School Health
http://www.cdc.gov/nccdphp/dash

CDC Division of Diabetes Translation
(877) 232-3422
http://www.cdc.gov/diabetes

CDC Division of Nutrition and Physical Activity
http://www.cdc.gov/nccdphp/dnpa

Diabetes Exercise and Sports Association
1647 B West Bethany Home Road
Phoenix, AZ 85015
(800) 898-4322
http://www.diabetes-exercise.org
This nonprofit service organization is dedicated to enhancing the quality of life for people with diabetes through exercise.

Disability Rights Education and Defense Fund (DREDF)
2212 Sixth Street
Berkeley, CA 94710
(510) 644-2555
http://www.dredf.org

DREDF is a national law and policy center dedicated to protecting and advancing the civil rights of people with disabilities through legislation, litigation, advocacy, technical assistance, and education and training of attorneys, advocates, persons with disabilities, and parents and children with disabilities.

Indian Health Service (IHS) National Diabetes Program
5300 Homestead Road, NE
Albuquerque, NM 87110
(505) 248-4182
http://www.ihs.gov
The mission of the IHS is to develop, document, and sustain a public health effort to prevent and control diabetes in American Indian and Alaskan Native communities.

Joslin Diabetes Center
1 Joslin Place
Boston, MA 02215
(800) 567-5461
http://www.joslin.harvard.edu
The Joslin Diabetes Center and its affiliates offer a full range of services for children and adults with diabetes, including programs to help youngsters with diabetes and their families better manage the disease.

Juvenile Diabetes Research Foundation International (JDRF)
120 Wall Street
New York, NY 10005-4001
(800) 533-2873
http://www.jdrf.org
The mission of JDRF is to find a cure for diabetes and its complications through the support of research.

Lawson Wilkins Pediatric Endocrine Society (LWPES)
867 Allardice Way
Stanford, CA 94305
(650) 494-3133
http://www.lwpes.org
The LWPES is a membership organization that promotes the acquisition and dissemination of knowledge of endocrine and metabolic disorders from conception through adolescence. The LWPES Web site provides links with information about diabetes in children and adolescents.

Lower Extremity Amputation Prevention Program
HRSA/BPH/DPSP
4350 East-West Highway, 9th Floor
Bethesda, MD 20814
(888) 275-4772
http://www.bphc.hrsa.gov/leap

National Center on Physical Activity and Disability (NCPAD)
1640 West Roosevelt Road
Chicago, IL 60608
(800) 900-8086
http://www.ncpad.org
The NCPAD provides information about current research, local programs, adapted equipment, recreation and leisure facilities, and many other aspects of physical activity for persons with disabilities, including children and adolescents with diabetes.

National Diabetes Education Program (NDEP)
1 Diabetes Way
Bethesda, MD 20892-3600
(800) 438-5383
http://www.ndep.nih.gov
The NDEP is a federally sponsored program of the National Institutes of Health and the Centers for Disease Control and Prevention, involving more than 200 public and private partners to improve diabetes treatment and outcomes for people with diabetes, promote early diagnosis, and prevent diabetes.

National Diabetes Information Clearinghouse (NDIC)
1 Information Way
Bethesda, MD 20892-3560
(800) 860-8747
http://www.niddk.nih.gov
The NDIC is a service of the National Institute of Diabetes and Digestive and Kidney Diseases that provides information about diabetes to people with diabetes, their families, health care professionals, and the public.

National Digestive Diseases Information Clearinghouse
2 Information Way
Bethesda, MD 20892-3570
(800) 891-5389

nddic@info.niddk.nih.gov
http://www.niddk.nih.gov/health/digest/nddic.htm

National Information Center for Children and Youth with Disabilities
P.O. Box 1492
Washington, DC 20013-1492
(800) 695-0285
http://www.nichcy.org
This national information and referral clearinghouse on special education and disability-related issues provides information about local, state, or national disability groups and gives technical assistance to parents and professionals.

National Institute of Child Health and Human Development (NICHD)
31 Center Drive, MSC 2425
Bethesda, MD 20892-2425
(301) 496-5133
http://www.nichd.nih.gov
The NICHD conducts and supports laboratory, clinical, and epidemiologic research on the reproductive, neurobiologic, developmental, and behavioral processes that determine and maintain the health of children, adults, families, and populations.

National Institutes of Diabetes and Digestive and Kidney Diseases (NIDDK)
Building 31, Room 9A06
31 Center Drive, MSC 2560
Bethesda, MD 20892-2560
(301) 496-3583
http://www2.niddk.nih.gov
The NIDDK conducts and supports research on many of the most serious diseases affecting public health. It supports much of the clinical research on the diseases of internal medicine and related subspecialty fields as well as many basic science disciplines.

National Kidney and Urologic Diseases Information Clearinghouse
3 Information Way
Bethesda, MD 20892-3580
(800) 891-5390
nkudic@info.niddk.nih.gov
http://www.niddk.nih.gov/health/kidney/nkudic.htm

Pediatric Endocrinology Nursing Society (PENS)
P.O. Box 2933
Gaithersburg, MD 20886-2933
(800) 723-2902
http://www.pens.org
PENS is a nonprofit professional nursing organization with the goal of advancing pediatric endocrine nursing. Its Web site features articles about diabetes-related topics, including insulin pump therapy, obesity in children, and development of a pediatric diabetes education program for home health nurses.

Pedorthic Footwear Association
7150 Columbia Gateway Drive, Suite G
Columbia, MD 21046-1151
(800) 673-8447
(410) 381-7278
http://www.pedorthics.org

U.S. Department of Agriculture (USDA)

Center for Nutrition Policy and Promotion
http://www.usda.gov/cnpp

Food and Nutrition Information Center
http://www.nal.usda.gov/fnic

Food and Nutrition Service
http://www.fns.usda.gov/fns
The USDA supports several programs of importance to students with diabetes: the Center for Nutrition Policy and Promotion, the Food and Nutrition Information Center, and the Food and Nutrition Service.

GLOSSARY

acanthosis nigricans A skin condition that often appears as a symptom of diabetes, characterized by brown velvety patches in the body folds.

acetone A chemical formed in the blood when the body uses fat instead of sugar (glucose) for energy. Its presence usually indicates that the body's cells don't have enough insulin or can't use the insulin that's there. Acetone passes through the body into the urine. Excess acetone can make someone's breath smell fruity.

acidosis Too much acid in the body. For a person with diabetes, this can lead to diabetic ketoacidosis.

adrenal glands Two organs above the kidneys that produce hormones, such as adrenalin, which along with insulin, control the body's use of glucose.

adult-onset diabetes A former term for Type 2 diabetes.

advanced glycation end products (AGEs) A group of compounds that may have a role in some diabetes complications (such as eye and nerve problems), although experts do not yet know whether the AGEs cause or are a result of diabetic complications.

alpha cell A type of cell in the islets of Langerhans in the pancreas that produces a hormone called glucagon, which boosts the level of sugar in the blood.

alternate site testing Using other parts of the body besides the fingertip to obtain blood for blood glucose testing.

amino acid The building blocks of proteins. Insulin is made of 51 amino acids.

angiopathy A disease of the blood vessels characterized by sluggish blood, which appears in patients with chronic diabetes. This slowed blood flow eventually harms the body's cells (such as those in the center of the eye), because they don't get enough blood.

antibodies Proteins the body uses to protect itself from foreign substances. When the body makes proteins against itself, these proteins are called autoantibodies.

antigen A substance that triggers the body to mount an immune defense, because the body interprets these substances as harmful. The body produces antibodies to fight the antigens.

arteriosclerosis A group of diseases characterized by thickened, hardened artery walls, slowing blood flow, which often develops in people who have had diabetes for a long time.

artificial pancreas A large machine used in hospitals to constantly measure glucose in the blood and that then releases the correct amount of insulin.

Aspartame An artificial sweetener used in place of sugar because it has very few calories and is safe for people with diabetes.

atherosclerosis One of many diseases in which fat builds up in the large- and medium-sized arteries, slowing down or stopping blood flow, that can happen to people who have had diabetes for a long time.

autoimmune disease A process in which the body's immune system mistakenly attacks and destroys body tissue it mistakes as foreign. Type 1 diabetes is considered to be an autoimmune disease because the patient's immune system attacks and destroys the insulin-producing beta cells in the pancreas.

autonomic neuropathy A disease of the nerves that affects the internal organs, such as the cardiovascular system, the digestive tract, and the genital organs, all nerves that cannot be consciously controlled.

basal/bolus insulin administration Using several daily injections of fast-acting insulin at mealtimes (the bolus doses) with one or more daily injections of long-acting insulin (the basal doses) to control blood sugar much like the way insulin pumps are used.

basal rate A continuous supply of low levels of insulin, as in insulin pump therapy.

beta cell A type of cell in the part of the pancreas called the islets of Langerhans that produces and releases insulin.

bladder A hollow organ into which urine drains from the kidneys.

blood glucose The main sugar the body produces for fuel, by breaking down proteins, fats, and carbohydrates (primarily from carbohydrates). Glucose enters cells with the help of insulin.

blood glucose monitoring Testing to see how much sugar is in the blood. To do this, a drop of blood is drawn from the fingertip and placed on the tip of a testing strip, which changes color depending on how much sugar is in the blood. The strip is read by comparing it to a chart, or it is inserted into a digital meter.

blood-sampling devices A small instrument for pricking the skin with a fine needle to obtain a sample of blood to test for sugar.

bolus An extra boost of insulin used to make up for an expected rise in blood sugar, such as the rise that occurs after eating.

borderline diabetes An old-fashioned term that is no longer used.

brittle diabetes An outdated term once used to describe diabetes that was very difficult to control. It is not a distinct form of diabetes and usually will respond to a more intensive team approach to care.

CDE See CERTIFIED DIABETES EDUCATOR.

capillary The smallest of the body's blood vessels, which may become weakened in people who have had diabetes for a long time.

capsaicin A substance derived from hot peppers that is the active ingredient in the creams used to relieve the pain of peripheral neuropathy.

carbohydrate A large class of organic compounds that includes simple carbohydrates (sugars and fruit) and complex carbohydrates (vegetables and starches) that the body breaks down into glucose (a simple sugar that the body can use for fuel) or to make glycogen, which is stored in the liver and muscles for future use. If the body lacks insulin or can't use the insulin it has (the basic problems in diabetes), it won't be able to use carbohydrates for energy the way it should.

carpal tunnel syndrome A nerve disorder affecting the hand that may occur in people with diabetes.

cataract Clouding of the lens of the eye that is fairly common among the elderly. In people with diabetes, this condition is sometimes referred to as a "sugar cataract."

certified diabetes educator (CDE) A health professional certified by the National Certification Board for Diabetes Educators to teach people with diabetes how to manage their condition. To earn this certification, an educator must have a degree in the health professions such as RN (nursing), MD or DO (physicians), RD (dieticians), R.Ph. or Pharm.D. (pharmacists), or MSW (social workers). In addition, the applicant must have had at least two years' experience in diabetes education and passed a comprehensive examination covering the field. Certified Diabetes Educators must be recredentialed every five years.

cholesterol A fatty substance found in blood, muscle, liver, brain, and other tissues that can build up in the walls of the larger arteries, causing a disease called atherosclerosis. Cholesterol is composed of HDL-cholesterol (the "good" cholesterol) and LDL-cholesterol (the "bad" cholesterol). Although both cholesterol and fat are classified as "lipids" because they don't dissolve in water, cholesterol differs from fat in that it doesn't contain fatty acids and it can't be burned in the body for fuel. Fat, on the other hand, is the body's primary energy reserve.

corn A thickening of the skin of the feet or hands, usually caused by pressure against the skin.

cortisol One of several hormones made in the adrenal glands that is responsible for activating the immune system and metabolizing glucose.

coxsackie B4 virus A germ that has been shown to damage the beta cells of the pancreas in lab tests. This virus may be one cause of Type 1 diabetes.

C-peptide A substance that is released into the bloodsteam by the pancreas in equal amounts with insulin. Measuring the C-peptide levels will show how much insulin the body is producing.

dawn phenomenon A sudden rise in blood sugar levels in the early morning hours that sometimes occurs in people with Type 1 diabetes and rarely in people with Type 2 diabetes. People who have high levels of blood sugar in the mornings before eating may need to monitor their blood sugar during the night; if blood sugar levels are rising, adjustments in evening snacks or insulin dosages may be needed.

dehydration Significant loss of water from the body, which can be caused by a very high level of sugar in the urine, and is one of the causes of the symptoms of diabetes (excessive thirst).

delta cell A type of pancreatic cell in the islets of Langerhans that make somatostatin, a hormone that may control how beta cells produce insulin and how the alpha cells produce glucagon.

dextrose Another name for glucose, a simple sugar found in the blood, the body's main source of energy.

diabetes insipidus A disease of the pituitary gland or kidney, which is a different condition from diabetes mellitus. Diabetes insipidus is often called water diabetes to distinguish it from sugar diabetes (diabetes mellitus). Most people with the condition have most of the same signs as someone with diabetes mellitus: frequent urination, thirst, hunger, and weakness. However, they do not have sugar in the urine.

diabetes mellitus The medical name for Type 1 and Type 2 diabetes.

diabetes mellitus Type 1 A type of diabetes that typically occurs in childhood and is characterized by the complete lack of insulin. Type 1 can be subdivided into immune-mediated diabetes (Type 1A) and idiopathic diabetes (Type 1B). Immune-mediated diabetes (Type 1A) is caused by an immune-system controlled destruction of the insulin-producing beta cells of the pancreas. Idiopathic diabetes (Type 1B) has no known cause. Former names for Type 1 diabetes include insulin-dependent diabetes mellitus, juvenile diabetes, juvenile-onset diabetes, and ketosis-prone diabetes.

diabetes mellitus Type 2 A condition in which the body either makes too little insulin or can't use the insulin it does have to help convert blood sugar to energy. Type 2 diabetes may be controlled with diet, exercise, and weight loss; in some cases, oral medications and/or insulin injections may be required.

diabetic amyotrophy A disease of the nerves leading to the muscles that affects only one side of the body, most often in older men with mild diabetes.

diabetic coma A serious emergency in which a person loses consciousness because the blood sugar is either too low or too high. If the sugar level is too low, the person has hypoglycemia; if the level is too high, the person has hyperglycemia and may develop ketoacidosis.

diabetic dermopathy A characteristic skin disorder of round reddish lesions found in up to half of men and 30 percent of women with diabetes. They usually appear on the thigh or shin, but they may appear also on the scalp, forearm, and trunk.

diabetic ketoacidosis Severe, out-of-control diabetes caused by a complete lack of circulating insulin that requires emergency treatment. Ketoacidosis may occur because of illness, taking too little insulin, or getting too little exercise. As the body starts using stored fat for energy, ketone bodies (acids) build up in the blood, leading to ketoacidosis. Symptoms include nausea and vomiting, which can lead to dehydration, stomach pain, deep and rapid breathing, flushed face, dry skin and mouth, a fruity breath odor, a rapid and weak pulse, and low blood pressure. If the person is not given fluids and insulin right away, ketoacidosis can lead to coma and even death.

diabetic myelopathy Spinal cord damage found in some people with diabetes.

diabetic osteopathy Temporary loss of foot bone as seen in an X-ray.

diabetic retinopathy A disease of the small blood vessels of the retina that become swollen, leaking fluid into the center of the retina that can cause blurred vision and may progress to many tiny blood vessels growing out and across the eye, eventually bleeding into the center of the eye, causing impaired vision and blindness.

dietician An expert in nutrition who helps people with special health needs plan the kinds and amounts of foods to eat. A registered dietician (RD) has special qualifications and should be part of any diabetic health care team.

diuretic A drug that increases the flow of urine to rid the body of extra fluid.

edema A swelling or puffiness of some part of the body such as the ankles, caused by water or other body fluids that have collected in the cells.

electromyography (EMG) and nerve conduction velocity (NCV) studies Simultaneous tests using the same equipment that can diagnose neuropathy and check for nerve damage in patients with diabetes.

emergency medical identification Cards, bracelets, or necklaces with a written message used by people with diabetes or other medical problems to alert others in case of a medical emergency, such as a diabetic coma.

endocrine glands Glands (such as the pancreas that produces insulin) that release hormones into the bloodstream and that affect how the body uses food (metabolism).

endocrinologist A physician who treats people with problem endocrine glands. Diabetes is an endocrine disorder.

endogenous antibodies Type 1 diabetes occurs when the body attacks its own beta cells in the pancreas, destroying the ability to produce insulin. In people with diabetes, several different antibodies against normal tissues are found, including islet-cell antibodies (ICA's), anti-insulin antibodies (AIA's), and anti-GAD antibodies.

enzymes A special type of protein that helps the body's chemistry work better and more quickly. Each enzyme usually has its own chemical job to do, such as helping to change starch into sugar.

epinephrine One of several hormones made in the adrenal glands that helps the liver release sugar and limits the release of insulin from the pancreas and is responsible for some of the symptoms of low blood sugar, including anxiety, sweating, tremors, pale skin, nausea, and rapid heart beat.

euglycemia A normal level of glucose (sugar) in the blood.

exchange lists A grouping of foods by type to help people on special diets stay on the diet. Each group lists food in specific serving sizes. A person can exchange, trade, or substitute a food serving in one group for another food serving in the same group. The lists put foods in six groups: starch/bread, meat, vegetables, fruit, milk, and fats. Within a food group, each serving has about the same amount of carbohydrate, protein, fat, and calories.

fasting plasma glucose (FPG) A test for diabetes to determine how much sugar a person has in the blood. The blood test is usually done in the morning, after not eating for eight hours. The normal, nondiabetic range for fasting plasma glucose is less than 100 mg/dl (6.1 mmol/L). If the level is 126 mg/dl (7 mmol/L) or higher, it usually means the person has diabetes. The previous name for this test was fasting blood sugar.

fats One of the three main classes of foods and a source of energy for the body. Fats keep the skin healthy and serve as energy stores for the body. Saturated fats are solid at room temperature, come from animal food products (such as butter, lard, meat fat, solid shortening, palm oil, and coconut oil), and tend to raise the level of cholesterol in the blood. Unsaturated fats, including monounsaturated fats and polyunsaturated fats, are liquid at room temperature, come from plant oils such as olive, peanut, corn, cottonseed, sunflower, safflower, and soybean, and tend to lower the level of cholesterol in the blood.

fatty acids A basic unit of fat. When insulin levels are too low or there isn't enough sugar to use for energy, the body burns fatty acids for energy, which produces waste products known as ketone bodies that can cause the acid level in the blood to become too high, which may lead to life-threatening ketoacidosis.

fiber A substance found in foods that come from plants and which helps in digestion and may lower cholesterol and help control blood sugar. Soluble fiber is found in beans, fruits, and oat products, dissolves in water, and may help lower blood fats and blood sugar. Insoluble fiber found in whole-grain products and vegetables passes directly through the digestive system, helping to rid the body of waste products.

first phase insulin release Release of insulin into the bloodstream from the beta cell within a few minutes after the blood sugar level rises. This quick release is of insulin that was previously produced by the body and which was being stored in the beta cell.

food exchanges Replacing items from one food group with items from another, as a way to help people stay on special food plans.

fractional urine Urine collected for a certain period of time during 24 hours; usually from breakfast to lunch, from lunch to dinner, from dinner to bedtime, and from bedtime to first rising.

fructosamine A type of test that depends on the average blood sugar level during the past three weeks. The fructosamine test complements the glycohemoglobin test, since the two are different assessments of diabetes control.

fructose A calorie-containing sugar found in fruits, vegetables, and honey that is used to sweeten some diet foods.

galactose A calorie-containing sugar contained in milk products and sugar beets that is produced naturally by the body.

gangrene The death of body tissue typically caused by a loss of blood flow, especially in the legs and feet.

gastroparesis A type of nerve damage that affects the stomach so that food isn't digested correctly and doesn't move through the stomach normally, leading to vomiting, nausea, and bloating, and interfering with diabetes control.

gene The basic unit of heredity passed from parent to child.

gestational diabetes mellitus (GDM) A type of temporary diabetes mellitus that can occur during the second half of pregnancy, characterized by higher-than-normal blood sugar levels. Babies of these mothers are often larger than normal (typically weighing more than nine pounds). When the pregnancy ends, the mother's blood sugar level returns to normal in about 95 percent of all cases.

gland An organ that is specialized for producing and secreting certain fluids, either for use in the body or for excretion. There are two types of glands. The exocrine glands discharge their secretions via ducts, and the endocrine glands secrete hormones directly into the blood. The pancreas is an endocrine gland that releases insulin into the blood to help body cells absorb sugar from the blood.

glaucoma An eye disease associated with increased pressure within the eye that can damage the optic nerve, leading to vision problems and eventual blindness.

glucagon A hormone that raises the level of glucose (sugar) in the blood. The alpha cells in the islets of Langerhans, located in the pancreas, produce glucagon when levels of blood sugar in the body drop. Glucagon has the opposite effect of insulin, which is released after a meal to lower blood sugar. It boosts blood sugar levels by stimulating glycogen breakdown and glucose release by the liver. An injectable form of glucagon is available to treat severe insulin reactions. When injected, the glucagon boosts blood sugar levels within 30 minutes. Family members of people with insulin-dependent Type 1 diabetes should learn how to administer glucagon.

gluconeogenesis The formation of glucose (sugar) from protein within the liver, in response to lowered blood sugar. After eating, the liver stores surplus sugar as glycogen. Between meals, sugar is released from glycogen stores.

glucose A simple sugar found in the blood that provides the main source of fuel for the body. Glucose is one of the most important carbohydrates in human metabolism. Simple sugars such as fructose and galactose must first be converted to glucose by the liver so they can be used for energy. Glucose occurs naturally in food, and it's a major ingredient in honey and table sugar (sucrose). When used as a food additive, it is known as dextrose.

glucose tolerance test A diabetes test given in the morning before eating. After a blood sample is taken, the person drinks a sugary liquid, followed by second blood drawn one hour later, and a third an hour after that. The test reveals how well the body handles the glucose in the blood over a period of time.

glycemia A medical term that indicates the level of glucose (sugar) in the blood. Hyperglycemia refers to too much sugar in the blood; hypoglycemia is too little blood sugar.

glycemic index A ranking of foods based on their immediate effect on blood sugar levels. The index measures how much a person's blood sugar rises within two or three hours after a meal. Carbohydrates that break down quickly during digestion have the highest glycemic index.

glycemic response The effect of different foods on blood glucose (sugar) levels over a period of time. Some foods boost blood sugar levels more quickly than others containing the same amount of carbohydrates.

glycogen A substance made up of sugars that is stored in the liver and muscles, releasing sugar into the blood when needed by the body's cells. Glycogen is the major source of stored fuel in the body.

glycogenesis Also called glucogenesis, this is the process by which glycogen is formed from glucose (sugar).

glycohemoglobin test See GLYCOSYLATED HEMOGLOBIN TEST.

glycosuria (or glucosuria) The condition of having sugar in the urine.

glycosylated hemoglobin test (glycohemoglobin) This blood test measures a person's average blood sugar level for the two or three months preceding the test and complements a fructosamine test.

hormone A chemical released by certain cells that directs other cells in what to do. Insulin is a hormone produced by the beta cells in the pancreas that helps other cells absorb sugar that the body uses for fuel.

human insulin Man-made insulin that is similar to natural insulin produced by the body. Human insulin has been available since 1982.

hyperglycemia An excessive level of sugar in the blood, which is an indication of uncontrolled diabetes (either Type 1 or Type 2). Hyperglycemia occurs when the body doesn't have enough insulin or can't use the insulin it has to help cells absorb sugar, and its symptoms include thirst, dry mouth, and frequent urination.

hyperinsulinism Too much insulin in the blood. This term typically refers to a condition in which the body produces too much insulin.

hyperlipidemia Too much fat in the blood.

hypertension High blood pressure.

hypoglycemia Too little sugar in the blood. This occurs when a person with diabetes has injected too much insulin, not eaten enough food, or has exercised without eating enough. Symptoms include nervousness, shakiness, weakness, headache, blurred vision, and hunger. Ingesting small amounts of sugar in the form of sweet juice, soda, or sweet foods will usually improve symptoms within 10 to 15 minutes.

hypoglycemia unawareness A dangerous situation in which a drop in blood sugar is not recognized, which can quickly lead to unconsciousness.

hypotension A sudden drop in blood pressure, which may cause dizziness or fainting.

impaired glucose tolerance (IGT) Blood sugar levels that are higher than normal, but not high enough to be considered diabetes. People with IGT may or may not go on to develop diabetes. Former names for IGT were borderline, subclinical, chemical, or latent diabetes.

implantable insulin pump A small internal pump that delivers insulin in response to commands from a hand-held programmer device.

injection sites Places on the body where people can inject insulin most easily. These include the outer area of the upper arm, just above and below the waist (except the area right around the navel), the upper area of the buttock behind the hip bone, and the front midpoint of the thigh. These sites are typically rotated to prevent lumps or small dents (lipodystrohies) from forming in the skin. However, the same body area should be used for injections given at the same time each day, to lessen the chance that insulin's action won't be the same.

insulin A hormone that helps the body's cells absorb sugar. The beta cells in the islets of Langerhans in the pancreas produce the insulin. If the body can't produce enough insulin, it must be injected. Insulin is either of recombinant DNA origin or pork-derived, semisynthetic origin.

insulin allergy A sensitivity to insulin made from pork or beef or from bacteria, or because the insulin is not the same as human insulin. The allergy can cause red, itchy skin around the injection site (local allergy) or a more serious systemic allergy, triggering hives or red patches all over the body and altered heartbeat and breathing. A doctor may treat this allergy by prescribing purified insulins or by desensitization.

insulin analog A synthetic modification of insulin that substitutes specific amino acids for natural ones. There are four insulin analogs sold in the United States: insulin lispro (Humalog), insulin aspart (Novolog/NovoRapid), insulin glargine (Lantus), and detemir (Levemir).

insulin antagonist A substance that fights the action of insulin. For example, insulin lowers the blood sugar level, and glucagon raises it; therefore, glucagon is an antagonist of insulin.

insulin binding When insulin attaches itself to something else, such as the outer part of a cell, allowing the cell to absorb sugar where it can be used for energy. If insulin binds with the proteins designed to protect the body from outside substances (antibodies), the body may then see injected insulin (not made by the body) as a "foreign" substance. When the injected insulin binds with the antibodies, it doesn't work as well as when it binds directly to the cell.

insulin-dependent diabetes mellitus Another name for Type 1 diabetes.

insulin-induced atrophy Small indentations in the skin that appear after repeated injections to the same spot.

insulin-induced hypertrophy Small lumps under the skin that occur after repeated injections in the same spot.

insulinoma A tumor of the beta cells in the islets of Langerhans in the pancreas. Although not usually malignant, these tumors may still cause the body to produce extra insulin, which may lead to a low blood sugar level.

insulin pen An insulin injection device that can be used instead of syringes for giving insulin injections.

insulin pump A battery-powered device that delivers a continuous supply of short-acting insulin, from the pump through a plastic catheter connected to a needle inserted into the skin. It can be manually set or preprogrammed to deliver a low, steady rate (basal rate) for day-long coverage, with extra boosts of insulin (bolus doses) to cover meals or when extra insulin is needed. No available pump can both measure the sugar level and calculate what changes to make in the insulin doses. The pump is usually used by people with insulin-dependent diabetes.

insulin reaction Another name for hypoglycemia (low levels of blood sugar).

insulin receptors Areas on the outside of a cell that allow the cell to bind with insulin to help the cell absorb sugar from the blood.

insulin resistance A condition in which insulin in the body does not work well enough to allow cells to absorb enough sugar from the blood. Many people with Type 2 diabetes produce enough insulin, but their bodies don't respond to insulin correctly because the person is overweight and doesn't respond well to insulin, or because the person is older (aging cells lose some of the ability to respond to insulin). Insulin resistance is also linked to high blood pressure and high levels of fat in the blood. Another kind of insulin resistance may sometimes happen in people taking insulin injections, who require very high doses of insulin every day to normalize their blood sugar.

insulin sensitizer Any of several diabetes medications that reduce insulin resistance, including metformin (Glucophage) and the thiazolidinediones rosiglitazone (Avandia) and pioglitazone (Actos).

insulin shock A former term for insulin reaction that is no longer used.

intensive management A type of treatment for Type 1 diabetes in which blood sugar levels are kept as close to normal as possible. This requires three or more insulin injections a day or an insulin pump; four or more blood sugar tests a day; adjustments of insulin, diet, and activity based on test results; dietary counseling; and diabetes team management.

intramuscular injection Injecting medication or fluids into a muscle.

intravenous injection Injecting medication or fluid directly into a vein.

islet cell antibodies (ICAs) Specialized islet cell proteins called antibodies that are found in the blood of many people with Type 1 diabetes. These antibodies are apparently released after damage to the beta cells of the pancreas, which makes their appearance an indicator that the autoimmune process has started. The antibodies that are presently routinely tested include IAA antiinsulin, GAD65 anti glutamic acid decarboxylase, ICA512 a specific islet cell antibody, EMA antiendomyseal antibodies, and anti 21-hydroxylase.

islet cells Clumps of cells in the pancreas that include cells that produce insulin. The cells include several subvarieties, including alpha cells (that produce glucagon), beta cells (producing insulin), and delta cells (producing somatostatin). They also include PP cells and D1 cells, which experts know little about.

islet cell transplantation Transplanting beta (islet) cells from a donor pancreas into a person whose pancreas has stopped producing insulin. Beta cells produce the insulin that the body needs to help cells absorb sugar for energy. Although transplanting islet cells may one day be a helpful treatment for diabetes, the procedure is still experimental. Transplantation of the pancreas itself is possible and is sometimes advised.

ketoacidosis See DIABETIC KETOACIDOSIS.

ketones (ketone bodies) Chemicals produced by the body when a lack of insulin requires the breakdown of fat to provide energy. As the ketones build up in the blood, they spill over into the urine so they can be removed. Another type of ketone (acetone) is expelled through the lungs, giving the breath a characteristic fruity odor. Ketones that build up in the body for a long time lead to serious illness and coma.

ketonuria The presence of ketone bodies in the urine, which is a warning sign of diabetic ketoacidosis.

ketosis A buildup of ketone bodies in body tissues and fluids, leading to nausea, vomiting, and stomach pain. Ketosis can lead to ketoacidosis.

labile diabetes See BRITTLE DIABETES.

lactic acidosis The buildup of lactic acid in the body. Cells produce lactic acid when they use sugar for energy, but if lactic acid accumulates in the body, it causes deep and rapid breathing, vomiting, and stomach pain. Lactic acidosis can be caused by diabetic ketoacidosis and is also a rare side effect of the diabetes medication metformin.

lactose A type of sugar found in milk and milk products that is considered a nutritive sweetener.

latent diabetes The former term for impaired glucose tolerance.

lente insulin A type of intermediate-acting insulin.

lipid Another term for fat. The body stores fat so that when it needs energy, it can break down the lipids into fatty acids and burn them. The two most commonly measured kinds of lipids are triglycerides and cholesterol.

lipoatrophy See LIPODYSTROPHY.

lipodystrophy Lumps (lipohypertrophy) or depressions (lipoatrophy) below the surface of the skin that appear as a result of continual injections into the same spot. Both forms of lipodystrophies (lumps and depressions) are harmless. People can lessen the risk of this problem by rotating the injection sites. Using purified insulins also may help.

lipohypertrophy See LIPODYSTROPHY.

lispro insulin An insulin analog that acts faster than regular insulin. It can be injected right before a meal, unlike regular insulin, which should be injected at least 30 minutes before a meal.

macrosomia A term meaning "large body" that refers to a larger-than-normal baby, which occurs when the mother's blood sugar levels have been higher than normal during the pregnancy. This is a preventable complication of gestational diabetes.

macular edema Swelling in the area near the center of the retina of the eye (the macula) that is responsible for reading vision. This is a common complication of diabetic retinopathy.

maturity-onset diabetes The former term for Type 2 diabetes.

maturity-onset diabetes of the young (MODY) A form of diabetes characterized by early onset (before age 25), autosomal dominant inheritance (that is, it is inherited by 50 percent of a parent's children) with diabetes in at least two generations of the patient's family.

Mauriac syndrome A condition that occurs because of chronic poor control of diabetes, leading to an enlarged liver as a result of excessive glycogen deposits. There is usually a history of repeated hospitalizations for ketoacidosis.

meal plan A guide for controlling the amount of calories, carbohydrates, fats, and proteins a person eats.

metabolic syndrome A combination of health conditions that place a person at high risk for heart disease. These conditions are Type 2 diabetes, high blood pressure, obesity, and high levels of fat in the blood. Some researchers believe that all of these conditions are associated with high insulin levels, and that the underlying problem in patients with metabolic syndrome is a problem with insulin release from the beta cells of the pancreas. It was previously known as Syndrome X.

metabolism The sum of all the chemical and physical changes in the body that enable its continued function. Metabolism involves the breadkdown of complex organic substances of the body, liberating energy needed for other processes. Insulin is necessary for the metabolism of food.

metformin A medication used to treat Type 2 diabetes, which belongs to a class of drugs called biguanides.

microalbumin Small amounts of protein in the urine that can't be detected by routine urinanalysis. Specialized dipsticks, or urine collections over a period of 12 to 24 hours, are used to measure the amount of microalbumin. If there is persistent microalbumin over several repeated tests at different times, there is a higher risk of diabetic nephropathy and macrovascular disease.

microaneurysm A small swelling on the side of tiny blood vessels that may break and bleed into nearby tissue. People with diabetes sometimes develop microaneurysms in the retina of the eye.

microvascular disease A problem of thickened, weakened blood vessels that sometimes occurs when a person has had diabetes for a long time. The blood vessels bleed, leak protein, and slow the flow of blood through the body, so that some cells (such as those in the center of the eye) don't get enough blood.

mixed dose The combination of two kinds of insulin in one injection; commonly, this involves mixing regular fast-acting insulin with a longer-acting insulin such as NPH. A mixed dose insulin schedule may be prescribed to provide both short-term and long-term coverage.

mononeuropathy A type of disease of the peripheral nerves in diabetes patients that affects a single nerve; the eye is a common site for this type of nerve damage.

nephrologist A doctor who specializes in the treatment of kidney diseases.

nephropathy Any disease of the kidneys. Kidney damage caused by diabetes is called diabetic nephropathy. The typical form of diabetic nephropathy is diabetic glomerulosclerosis, a slowly progressive condition characterized by large amounts of urine protein and high blood pressure. It usually doesn't occur until after many years of diabetes and can be delayed by tight control of the blood sugar. The best way to diagnose diabetic nephropathy early is to measure microalbumin in the urine.

nerve conduction velocity (NCV) studies and electromyography (EMG) Tests used to diagnose kidney disease and check for nerve damage, which are usually administered at the same time with the same equipment.

neuroglycopenic A shortage of sugar in the nerve cells of the brain. Since brain cells depend on sugar as their main fuel, low blood sugar can quickly lead to brain problems, such as a change in mental function with possible seizures or loss of consciousness.

neurologist A doctor who specializes in the treatment of diseases of the nervous system.

neuropathy Disease of the nervous system.

nocturnal hypoglycemia Low blood sugar that occurs while the patient is asleep (between the evening injection and arising). Symptoms include restlessness, nightmares, and profuse sweating.

noninvasive blood glucose monitoring A method of measuring blood sugar without having to prick a finger to obtain a blood sample.

nonketotic coma A complication of diabetes caused by dehydration and a lack of insulin. Symptoms include very high levels of sugar in the blood, absence of ketoacidosis, severe dehydration, and a sleepy, confused, or comatose state. Nonketotic coma is more commonly associated with Type 2 diabetes and is sometimes the first symptom. Nonketotic coma is not common in Type 1 diabetes.

NPH insulin A type of intermediate-acting insulin.

obesity A condition in which excess fat has accumulated in the body; typically, at least 20 percent extra body fat for a person's age, height, sex, and bone structure. Fat interferes with the action of insulin. Extra body fat is believed to be a risk factor for diabetes.

ophthalmologist A physician who diagnoses and treats people with eye diseases.

optometrist A person trained to test the eyes, prescribe, and fit corrective lenses and eyeglasses.

oral glucose tolerance test (OGTT) A test used to diagnose diabetes.

oral hypoglycemic agents Medications taken by mouth to lower the level of blood sugar in patients with Type 2 diabetes whose pancreases still produce some insulin. These medications include the sulfonylureas (many varieties), metformin (Glucophage), acarbose (Precose), miglitol (Glyset), rosiglitazone (Avandia), pioglitazone (Actos), repaglinide (Prandin), and nateglinide (Starlix).

pancreas An organ located behind the stomach and responsible for producing insulin and making enzymes that help the body digest food. Spread all over the pancreas are the islets of Langerhans, where alpha cells make glucagon, which raises the level of blood sugar, beta cells produce insulin, and delta cells produce somatostatin.

pancreas transplant A surgical procedure in which the pancreas of a person with diabetes is replaced with a healthy pancreas that can produce insulin. A person can donate half a pancreas and still live normally. Pancreas transplants are usually performed in patients with Type 1 diabetes who have severe complications.

pancreatectomy A procedure in which a surgeon removes the pancreas.

pancreatitis Inflammation of the pancreas, which can make the pancreas stop working. Pancreatitis is caused by excessive drinking, by gallbladder disease, or by a virus.

pediatric endocrinologist A physician who treats children who have problems of the endocrine glands, such as diabetes.

peptide Two or more amino acids linked together chemically. A very long string of amino acids is called a protein.

periodontal disease Disease of the gums. People who have diabetes are more likely to have gum disease.

periodontist A specialist in the treatment of diseases of the gums.

peripheral neuropathy Nerve damage, usually affecting the feet and legs, causing pain, numbness, or tingling. It is also sometimes called somatic neuropathy or distal sensory polyneuropathy.

peripheral vascular disease (PVD) Disease of the large blood vessels of the arms, legs, and feet. People who have had diabetes for a long time may be diagnosed with this disease, because major blood vessels in their arms, legs, and feet become blocked and their limbs don't receive enough blood. Symptoms include aching pains in the arms, legs, and feet, and foot sores that heal slowly. Taking good care of feet, avoiding smoking, and keeping blood pressure and diabetes under good control reduces the risk of PVD.

photocoagulation A treatment method for diabetic retinopathy in which a strong laser is used to seal off bleeding blood vessels in the eye.

pioglitazone A medication used to treat Type 2 diabetes that belongs to a class of drugs called thiazolidinediones.

podiatrist A physician who specializes in the care and treatment of feet.

point system A rarely used system of meal planning for diabetes in which foods are rated on calorie content, regardless of the effect on blood glucose or the nutritional content. In this system, one calorie point equals 75 calories. The system may help with weight loss, but is not presently recommended in the treatment of Type 1 diabetes.

polycystic ovary syndrome (PCOS) This condition is associated with cysts on both ovaries and insulin resistance. Symptoms frequently include decreased menstrual flow, irregular menses, lack of ovulation, and infertility.

polyunsaturated fats A type of fat that comes from vegetables.

polyuria Excessive urination; this may be a symptom of uncontrolled diabetes.

Poor Man's Pump See BASAL/BOLUS INSULIN ADMINISTRATION.

postprandial Occurring after a meal. For example, a blood test performed one or two hours after eating used to assess the amount of sugar in the blood would be called a postprandial blood glucose test.

prediabetes The state in which a person's blood sugar levels are higher than normal, but not high enough for a diagnosis of diabetes. Physicians sometimes call this condition impaired glucose tolerance or impaired fasting glucose (IGT/IFG), depending on which test was used to detect it.

preprandial Occurring before a meal. For example, a blood test performed before eating to measure the blood sugar is a preprandial blood glucose test.

previous abnormality of glucose tolerance (PrevAGT) A condition in which a person has had an above-normal level of blood sugar in the past, but who tests normal on a current test. PrevAGT used to be called either "latent diabetes" or "prediabetes."

proliferative retinopathy A disease of the small blood vessels of the retina of the eye.

protein One of the three main classes of food, proteins are made of amino acids. Cells need protein to grow and to repair themselves. Protein is found in many foods such as meat, fish, poultry, and eggs.

proteinuria Too much protein in the urine, which may be a sign of kidney damage.

pruritus The medical term for itching skin, which may be a symptom of diabetes.

purified insulins Insulins with much less of the impure proinsulin. Experts believe that using purified insulins may help avoid or reduce some of the problems of people with diabetes, such as allergic reactions.

reactive hypoglycemia A fall in blood sugar that causes symptoms right after a meal. Reactive hypoglycemia is different from spontaneous hypoglycemia, which is not associated with food. Reactive hypoglycemia generally is harmless.

rebound A swing to a high level of blood sugar after having a low level.

receptors Areas on the outer part of a cell that allow the cell to join or bind with insulin that is in the blood.

recommended dietary allowance (RDA) Recommendations for daily intake of specific nutrients for groups of healthy individuals set by the Food and Nutrition Board of the National Research Council of the National Academy of Science.

regular insulin A type of fast-acting insulin.

renal A term that pertains to the kidneys.

repaglinide (Prandin) A medication used to treat Type 2 diabetes and that belongs to a class of drugs called meglitinides.

renal glycosuria A large amount of sugar in the urine when there is a normal amount of sugar in the blood, due to an inherited inability of the kidneys to reabsorb sugar completely.

renal threshold When the blood contains so much of a substance (such as sugar) that the kidneys allow the excess to spill into the urine.

retina The center part of the back of the eye, responsible for sensing light. The many small blood vessels may be harmed when a person has had diabetes for a long time.

retinopathy A disease of the small blood vessels in the retina of the eye.

rosiglitazone (Avandia) A drug used as a treatment for Type 2 diabetes that belongs to a class of drugs called thiazolidinediones.

saccharin A man-made sweetener that people use in place of sugar because it has no calories.

saturated fat A type of fat that comes from animals.

secondary diabetes When someone develops diabetes because of another disease or as the result of taking certain drugs or chemicals.

second phase insulin release Delayed release of insulin into the bloodstream from the beta cell after the blood glucose level rises. It is thought that this delayed release is due to release of insulin that is manufactured in the beta cell after the blood sugar starts to rise.

segmental transplantation A surgical procedure in which a part of a pancreas that contains insulin-producing cells is transplanted into a person whose pancreas has stopped making insulin.

self-monitoring of blood sugar Testing of blood sugar at home, also called home blood sugar monitoring.

shock A serious condition that causes very low blood pressure, lower body temperature, and a decreased level of consciousness. Untreated shock can be fatal.

somatostatin A hormone made by the delta cells in the islets of Langerhans in the pancreas. This hormone may control the way in which the body secretes insulin and glucagon.

Somogyi effect A sudden spike in blood sugar from an extremely low to a high level. This typically happens after an untreated insulin reaction during the night.

sorbitol A sugar alcohol used in a wide range of foods and toothpastes, which can cause stomach distress and diarrhea in some individuals. It contains four calories in every gram, the same as table sugar and starch. Too much sorbitol in cells can cause damage; diabetic retinopathy and nerve damage may be related to too much sorbitol in the cells of the eyes and nerves.

spilling point The point at which the blood contains so much of a substance such as sugar that the kidneys allow the excess to spill into the urine.

split dose The division of a prescribed daily dose of insulin into two or more injections to be taken during the day. Many people who use insulin believe that multiple injections allow more consistent control over blood sugar levels.

stiff hand syndrome A condition that occurs only in people with diabetes in which the skin of the palm thickens so that the hand cannot be held in a straight position.

subclinical diabetes An outdated term for impaired glucose tolerance.

subcutaneous injection An injection of medication or fluids into the tissue under the skin.

sucrose Simple table sugar. This form of sugar must be broken down in the body into a more simple form before the blood can absorb it and send it into the cells.

sugar A sweet-tasting type of carbohydrate that can be used quickly and easily by the body as fuel. Types of sugar include lactose, glucose, fructose, and sucrose.

sulfonylureas One of several different classes of pills that lower the blood level of sugar in patients with Type 2 diabetes. There are several different types of sulfonylureas available. The four first-generation sulfonylureas have been prescribed for some time; the three second-generation drugs have been recently developed. The second-generation drugs are more potent and carry fewer side effects. The first-generation medications include tolbutamide (Orinase), acetohexamide (Dymelor), tolazamide (Tolinase), and chloropropamide (Diabinese). The second-generation medications are glipizide (Glucotrol, Glucotrol XL), glyburide (Diabeta, Micronase, Glynase), and glimepiride (Amaryl).

syndrome A combination of signs or symptoms that form a distinct clinical picture of a particular condition, disorder, or disease.

syndrome X The old-fashioned phrase (more correctly called metabolic syndrome) describing a combination of health conditions that place a person at high risk for heart disease. These conditions include Type 2 diabetes, obesity, high blood pressure, and high levels of fat in the blood. Many scientists believe that all these symptoms are associated with high blood insulin levels and that the underlying problem in patients with syndrome X may be the impaired insulin release from the beta cells of the pancreas.

thiazolidinediones One of several different classes of pills used by patients with Type 2 diabetes that lower the blood sugar level, also called "glitazones." The thiazolidinediones include rosiglitazone (Avandia) and pioglitazone (Actos).

thrush An infection of the mouth that may be a problem for people with diabetes, when high levels of sugar in mouth fluids encourages the growth of fungus. Symptoms are patches of whitish-colored skin in the mouth.

thyroid An endocrine gland in the neck that produces two hormones that regulate the body's metabolic rate (T4 and T3, also called thyroxine and triiodothyronine—or more simply, thyroid hormone). Overactivity of the thyroid gland is called hyperthyroidism; underactivity is called hypothyroidism. Both hyperthyroidism and hypothyroidism may be an autoimmune problem, and both are more common in people with Type 1 diabetes.

thyroid stimulating hormone (TSH) A hormone secreted by the anterior pituitary gland that controls the production and release of the thyroid hormones T3 and T4. Measurement of the TSH blood level is a common screening tool for hypothyroidism and hyperthyroidism and issued to assess whether treatment is working for people with these conditions. Typically, high values of TSH are associated with hypothyroidism, and absence of TSH is linked to hyperthyroidism.

tolazamide An oral hypoglycemic medication taken to lower the blood sugar level in people with Type 2 diabetes.

tolbutamide An oral hypoglycemic medication taken to lower the blood sugar level in people with Type 2 diabetes.

transcutaneous electronic nerve stimulation (TENS) A treatment for painful nerve damage.

triglyceride A type of fat in the blood. The body needs insulin to remove this type of fat from the blood. When a patient's diabetes is under control and their weight is normal, the level of triglycerides in the blood is also typically normal.

troglitazone An oral hypoglycemic medication formerly used as a treatment for Type 2 diabetes that belonged to a class of drugs called thiazolidinediones. Troglitazone was withdrawn from the market in 2000 because of rare liver problems.

twenty-four hour urine The total amount that a person urinates in a 24-hour period.

ultralente insulin A type of long-acting insulin.

unit of insulin The basic measure of insulin. U-100 insulin means 100 units of insulin per milliliter (ml) or cubic centimeter (cc) of solution. Most insulin produced today in the United States is U-100.

unsaturated fat A type of fat that contains a fairly high percentage of fatty acids. Fish oils and most vegetable fats are unsaturated, as opposed to animal fats and shortening, which are saturated. Unsaturated fats are liquid at room temperature. Unsaturated fats fall into two groups—monounsaturated and polyunsaturated fats. Olive oil is a monounsaturated fat, which seems to lower the risk of heart disease by lowering cholesterol while keeping levels of HDL (good) cholesterol high. Polyunsaturated fats include corn and soybean oil.

unstable diabetes An outdated term for a type of diabetes characterized by quickly fluctuating blood sugar levels, also formerly known as brittle diabetes or labile diabetes.

urea One of the chief waste products of the body that results from the breakdown of food in the body. The kidneys flush the waste from the body in the form of urea, which is in the urine.

urine testing Checking urine to see if it contains sugar and ketones by placing special strips of paper or tablets (called reagents) into a small amount of urine. Changes in the color of the strip reveal how much sugar or ketones are present in the urine. Urine testing is the only way to check for the presence of ketones, which is a sign of serious illness, but urine testing is less effective than blood testing in monitoring blood sugar levels.

xylitol A sugar alcohol used as a sweetener; small amounts are found in strawberries, raspberries, plums, and vegetables such as eggplant and cauliflower. Xylitol is as sweet as table sugar (sucrose). Xylitol is used in sugar-free gum and in some diet foods, such as jams and jellies. It has little effect on blood sugar.

READ MORE ABOUT IT

GENERAL INFORMATION

Freeman, Charlene. *Practical Guide for Reaching Diabetes Target Goals.* Eau Claire, Wis.: PESI HealthCare, 2003.

Roszler, Janis, William H. Polonsky, and Steven V. Edelman. *The Secrets of Living and Loving with Diabetes: Three Experts Answer Questions You've Always Wanted to Ask.* Chicago: Surrey Books, 2004.

BLOOD SUGAR

Brand-Miller, Jennie, Kaye Foster-Powell, and Rick Mendosa. *What Makes My Blood Glucose Go Up . . . And Down? And 101 Other Frequently Asked Questions about Your Blood Glucose Levels.* New York: Marlowe & Company, 2003.

COOKING

Betty Crocker's Diabetes Cookbook: Everyday Meals, Easy as 1-2-3. Minneapolis, Minn.: Betty Crocker, 2003.

Glick, Ruth, and Nancy Baggett. *One Pot Meals for People with Diabetes.* Alexandria, Va.: American Diabetes Association, 2002.

Schiller, Eric. *The Official Pocket Guide to Diabetic Exchanges.* Alexandria, Va.: American Diabetes Association, 2003.

Schneider, Clara G. *The Diabetic's Brand Name Food Exchange Handbook.* Philadelphia: Running Press, 1991.

Warshaw, Hope S. and Nancy S. Hughes. *The Diabetes Food and Nutrition Bible: A Complete Guide to Planning, Shopping, Cooking, and Eating.* Alexandria, Va.: American Diabetes Association, 2001.

Woodruff, Sandra. *The Good Carb Cookbook: Secrets of Eating Low on the Glycemic Index.* New York: Avery, 2001.

DIABETES CAMP

Getting the Most Out of Diabetes Camp: A Guide for Parents and Kids. Edited by the American Diabetes Association. Alexandria, Va.: American Diabetes Association, 2002.

DIABETES PILLS

Whitaker, Julian. *Reversing Diabetes: Reduce or Even Eliminate Your Dependence on Insulin or Oral Drugs.* New York: Warner Books, 2001.

EXERCISE

Colberg, Sheri. *The Diabetic Athlete.* Champaign, Ill.: Human Kinetics Publishers, 2000.

Hayes, Charlotte. *The I Hate to Exercise Book for People with Diabetes.* Alexandria, Va.: American Diabetes Association, 2001.

Holzmeister, Lee Ann. *The Diabetes Carbohydrate and Fat Gram Guide: Quick, Easy Meal Planning Using Carbohydrate and Fat Gram Counts.* Alexandria, Va.: American Diabetes Association, 2000.

Hornsby, W. Guyton. *The Fitness Book: For People with Diabetes.* Alexandria, Va.: American Diabetes Association, 1996.

Ruderman, Neil, John T. Devlin, Stephen H. Schneider, and Andrea M. Kriska, eds. *Handbook of Exercise in Diabetes.* Alexandria, Va.: American Diabetes Association, 2001.

GLYCEMIC INDEX

Brand-Miller, Jennie. *The New Glucose Revolution Life Plan (New Glucose Revolution Series).* New York: Marlowe & Company, 2004.

———. *The New Glucose Revolution Pocket Guide to Losing Weight.* New York: Marlowe & Company, 2003.

———. *The New Glucose Revolution Pocket Guide to Diabetes.* New York: Marlowe & Company, 2003.

———. *The New Glucose Revolution: The Authoritative Guide to the Glycemic Index—the Dietary Solution for Lifelong Health.* New York: Marlowe & Company, 2002.

INSULIN

Goldstein, Barry. *Think Like a Pancreas: A Practical Guide to Managing Diabetes with Insulin.* New York: Marlowe & Company, 2004.

Whitaker, Julian. *Reversing Diabetes: Reduce or Even Eliminate Your Dependence on Insulin or Oral Drugs.* New York: Warner Books, 2001.

INSULIN PUMPS

Scheiner, Gary. *Insulin Pump Therapy Demystified: An Essential Guide for Everyone Pumping Insulin.* New York: Marlowe & Company, 2002.

Walsh, John. *Pumping Insulin: Everything You Need for Success with an Insulin Pump.* San Diego: Torrey Pines Press, 2000.

Wolpert, Howard. *Smart Pumping: A Practical Approach to the Insulin Pump.* Alexandria, Va.: American Diabetes Association, 2002.

MENTAL AND SPIRITUAL HEALTH

Caring for the Diabetic Soul. Edited by the American Diabetes Association. Alexandria, Va.: American Diabetes Association, 1997.

Creekmore, Charles. *Zen and the Art of Diabetes Maintenance: A Complete Field Guide for Spiritual and Emotional Well-Being.* Alexandria, Va.: American Diabetes Association, 2002.

Feste, Catherine. *Meditations on Diabetes: Strengthening Your Spirit in Every Season.* Alexandria, Va.: American Diabetes Association, 1999.

Polonsky, William H. *Diabetes Burnout: Preventing It, Surviving It, Finding Inner Peace.* Alexandria, Va.: American Diabetes Association, 1999.

Rubin, Richard L. *Psyching Out Diabetes: A Positive Approach to Your Negative Emotions.* New York: McGraw-Hill, 1999.

PREVENTION

Becker, Gretchen, and Allison B. Goldfine. *Prediabetes: What You Need to Know to Keep Diabetes Away.* New York: Marlowe & Company, 2005.

Saudek, Christopher. *The Complete Diabetes Prevention Plan.* New York: Avery, 2004.

TEENS AND KIDS WITH DIABETES

Betschart-Roemer, Jean. *In Contro: A Guide for Teens with Diabetes.* New York: Wiley, 1995.

Loy, Bo, and Spike Loy. *487 Really Cool Tips for Kids with Diabetes.* Alexandria, Va.: American Diabetes Association, 2004.

Loy, Spike, and Virginia Loy. *Getting a Grip on Diabetes: Quick Tips for Kids and Teens.* Alexandria, Va.: American Diabetes Association, 2000.

WEIGHT LOSS

Daly, Anne, Judith Wylie-Rosett, and Linda Delehanty. *101 Weight Loss Tips for Preventing and Controlling Diabetes.* Alexandria, Va.: American Diabetes Association, 2002.

Maggi, Annette, and Jackie Boucher. *What You Can Do to Prevent Diabetes: Simple Changes to Improve Your Life.* New York: Wiley, 2000.

Walsh, John, Ruth Roberts, Timothy Bailey, and Chandra B. Varma. *Using Insulin, Everything You Need for Success with Insulin.* San Diego: Torrey Pines Press, 2003.

INDEX

C

D

E

F

O

P

Q

R